Copyright © 2009 Sofía B. Jaimes
All rights reserved. No part of this book may be
reproduced or utilized in any form or by any
means without written permission from the author.
ISBN: 978-0-615-33787-6
Book Design by Norman Ibarra
Cover photograph by Bruna Zavattiero © www.brunazavattiero.it
Images by Jorge Bonnet Belmontes

Visit our website: sofiatwins.com

Twins
Seeing double

Tales from the heart
of a mother of twins

By Sofía B. Jaimes

Contents

I Don't Fit 11
In My Kingdom 15
Welcome 17
Mirrors 21
Thirty-Six 25
Visiting during Christmas 29
Having Twins 35
Has Anyone Seen My Babies? 39
Homemade Dwarves 43
Do You Remember? 47
Toddler Twins 53
My Fantasy House 57
Bye-Bye Babies 63
She is Having Twins 67
La Bacinica (Or On Potty Training) 71
Are We The Only Ones? 75
The Old Me 79
I Choose You 83
Missing Them Already 87
Reborn 91
Saturday In Darien 95
Wild Flowers 101
There Is Hope 105
Sad Iron 111
Beds 115
Lies 119
The End of the Honeymoon 125
Fever 131
Don't Grow 135
Gracias 139
Going to Kindergarten 143

Dedication

I dedicate this book to all mothers of twins. They are my heroes because they have raised two at a time, when nature originally intended women to have one at a time. Because only they know how difficult raising twins can be, how extraordinarily challenging and satisfying at the same time. To them I dedicate this humble selection of my own experiences as a mother of twins.

Many great books have been written about twins in the past decade. Many of them give wonderful advice and have lists of recommendations on what to do when you have twins. This book is different. This book is about the emotions you will go through when you have twins. In those very few moments when our boys were babies that I could, I sneaked some time to write. I needed to write so badly. My emotions were going amok, I felt my feelings were totally exposed, one moment I was deliriously happy, the next I was so overwhelmed. I had to write. I had no option. It was my only way to put context around our world then and it allowed me to make sense of it. When I saw the babies lock their eyes for the first time on mine, when they touched my face with their minute hands, when I saw my husband carry them with such tenderness – I had to write. It was an impulse that I often had to constrain because there were priorities: diapers needed to be changed, laundry washed, phone calls returned, I actually had to make time to sit down and eat myself. But our boys were as cute as all babies are, and inevitably charmed us, seduced us with their giggles, made us mad with their demands. I felt I was going to explode at times because I had never experienced such joy and such distress at unison. Joy to be able to help these two little creatures grow, and distress for my own inability to let go – why can't babies stay little a bit longer?

Foreword

It is exactly that need to freeze the fascinating moments, good and bad, that fed my impulse to write these essays. They are short, you will be able to read them at intervals, because we all know when you are raising twins there is one thing that is always short: time!

Enjoy!

Sofía

Sofía B. Jaimes

Chapter 1

I Don't Fit

I don't fit in my clothes. They are too tight. I don't fit in my car. I have to slide the seat all the way back to be able to drive. I cannot climb up stairs like before because I get tired on the fourth step and I have to stop to catch my breath. I cannot carry things because they feel too heavy and my feet cannot take one more kilo. I cannot see my feet if I look down.

I don't live in my house, or in the gym, or in the office. Now I live in the bathroom going pee every two hours. I cannot stand work itself because I have lost interest in it. I cannot stand distance. All those kilometers that separate me from my family are killing me because they separate me from my family, my friends in Mexico City, Pittsburgh, Buenos Aires, Rio. I see planes and I want to climb on the first one flying by and ask the pilot to take me to see my loved ones, even if it is only for pity, because I cannot stand being alone. I want my belly to be rubbed constantly and I want to be pampered. I don't dream of having fun, now I dream of surgery rooms, things that get lost and bodies that open from places they normally don't. David does not fit in our bed anymore, because I need a lot of space to be comfortable and I need all those pillows surrounding me. Now the poor thing sleeps in the other room exiled from his own nuptial bed.

My rings don't fit in my fingers any longer. They go in, but cannot come off. I cannot reach my feet when I take a shower or when I want to put cream on my heels. I cannot be standing up for more than two minutes without starting to look for a place to sit. I do not eat like a normal person anymore. Now I eat each time my stomach rumbles, which could be every so often. I cannot put my socks on without moaning, and when I take off my pants I have to let them fall, and then twist myself in strange ways to pick them up. I cannot tie my tennis shoes either.

My back cannot take it anymore. It sends me messages that this must stop soon or it will crack. I cannot stand the anxiety for time to go by quickly, so that all by doubts and fears are forgotten, so that my body is back to its normal state, so I can come and go like before, do exercise, travel, breath deeply without tachycardia, so I can sleep eight hours uninterrupted, eat normally, go for a bike ride, ski, savor a good tequila, or a couple of glasses of wine, plan vacations, make love, cook for hours without looking at the clock, or without having to sit down every five minutes.

I want to be the Sofia I used to be; the one who wandered around with a lot of energy, the fearless one, invulnerable to worries, deceptions, sadness; the one who had everything under control and had an explanation for every single thing. Now I am a shred of emotions, the finale of my present situation terrorizes me. I have nightmares that my nipples rip in fours, I learn about girls who have abortions and that makes me cry, I watch the news that talks about the injustices in our world and I want to hide in the basement forever. I have doubts about everything, nothing is stable within or outside of me.

At the same time, I see everything differently, like a glass that makes me see things with a different color as if the things that were close and important, are now distant and trivial. And all those things that I considered dispensable are now extremely important. I cannot stand the idea that something happens to David, or to my sisters, brothers, my friends, mom or dad. I depend on them like I never depended on anyone. I am like a little girl who cannot walk alone and who needs help for everything: David cooks, helps me carry things, open doors for me, brings me cushions. David buys me milk, buys the groceries, does the dishes, does the laundry, cleans cars, fills and empties the pantry. And while I watch him, I feel him close and I cannot live without him. I don't want to live without him. Ever.

I don't fit in my plans or in the image that I used to have of myself. I look at myself in the mirror and there is someone else in it, watching me, all seems the same except for the roundness in my belly that makes me wonder if I ate the full moon one night… is that what happened to me?

So off we are on an unprecedented ride, us three, you two my little ones within me, and me piloting the vessel. Here I am, and I go with you. May we all arrive safe my dear sons.

"I look at myself in the mirror
and there is someone else
in it, watching me, all seems
the same except for the
roundness in my belly that
makes me wonder if I ate
the full moon one night...
is that what happened to me?"

In My Kingdom

Chapter 2

I live with two princes. One is ivory, the other one brown marble. One dies to sleep in my arms, the other one prefers his bed alone after he is satiated with me. One flees my eyesight to see the world and discover something new, famished to fill up of emotions unknown to him. The other one takes me to his adventures, he wants to share them with me, and holds my hand tight when something he discovers scares or confuses him.

For them, I am the queen, and they treat me with celestial adoration, but sometimes I am their maid and they mistreat me until they get what they want. I am the earth who gave birth to them; I am their homeland, their destiny.

They belong to a line of royalty unknown to us mortals, they were assigned by gods of the highest rank to come to our world to give us the opportunity to serve them... or at least that is what these princes believe. And so we laugh together, other times we cry, others we just hold each other and admire the marvel of being together in this precise point in time and space in which we coincide today. It does not matter if I am their subject or their princess; the only thing that matters is that we are together in this reign.

Chapter 3: Welcome

Thank you for coming to celebrate the baptism of Sebastián and Rodrigo. In this celebration, they are given a name and they are welcomed to our community. Both are very important for two little babies. Five months ago, they were born healthy and strong, and here they are today with their 16 and 18 pounds each, every single gram of joy and interest for the world they are just discovering. And you are all part of that world.

I would like all of you to join us in our wishes for our kids today:

Sebastián and Rodrigo,
May your smiles be with you all your life. Even in the face of sadness and disappointment, may you keep a good sense of humor. May your interest in discovering your world never end, always searching for new ways, new horizons that amaze you. May you marvel on Nature and may you learn to respect her. We wish you strength of will and compassion, never look back if you have to say good-bye, and welcome all the warmth and love others have to give you. Be thankful for what you have: health in your mind and body, caring people around you and bread on your table. Do grow up to respect and honor your ancestors, they came from far away countries like Poland, Mexico, France, Spain and England. You are a condensed version of dozens of generations of people with very different backgrounds, and they are now merged in you, and may their good attributes show in your characters to help you be happy and content with life. When you fail or make mistakes, always remember that that is a part of learning, and be proud of whom you are, because if you are honest and kind, good things will always come in your way, rest assured of that. May the joy you are bringing to us every day be returned to you exponentially.

You have been together since your conception. So far, you have shared everything: womb, love, attention, clothes, time. Continue this sharing and be good friends all your life, partners and accomplices in the good and the bad. May you make the best of being twins and may you also be strong at facing the challenge of being labeled as one, since you are also individuals that like to be treated as such. Always care and look out for each other, forever.

Today, all these friends and family are here to wish you the best in life. May you grow to thank them for that. Welcome, Sebastián and Rodrigo, to our world and our lives.

"You have been together since your conception. So far, you have shared everything: womb, love, attention, clothes, time. Continue this sharing and be good friends all your life, partners and accomplices in the good and the bad."

Chapter 4

Mirrors

Today we went to the new twin mothers' party at Allison's house. There were more than 20 pairs of twins, ranging from 10 weeks to maybe 8 or 9 years old. What a mix of identical faces, little skirts, and shorts of the same color! That garden was full of mirrors, mobile mirrors, which ran from one place to the next, following one another, getting wet in the little pool, rolling in the grass like there was no yesterday, no tomorrow, no day before yesterday nor next year; only today. All the boys and girls permanently by their sister or brother who is always there, always sharing life, toys, adventures, wonder looks, meals and their parents' love.

There were a set of twins, two and a half months, so little, fragile, sweet as cotton candy. There were two twin girls dressed in yellow, cheeks like apples, eyes like blue marbles, curly hair that floated with them while they ran one after the other one, illuminated by a splendorous sun: the one from up above and the one that they irradiate to each other with mutual love.

There were mothers that by raising two at the same time, know how to do everything at the same time: they talk, rub a bruise, eat, decide, look with their eyes for the other twin, everything instantaneously. The mother of the baby twins had several arms to help her carry and feed them, and she was liberated for a little while of the unstoppable task which is to have one baby, or the other, in arms *all the time* in the first months, feeding them, changing them, burping them or simply hugging them to protect them from the future which is not always as bright as that day. I saw a mother of twin girls eight months old, both dressed in pink and white, chubby, beautiful, that ate at the same time, cried at the same time, slept at the same time. I ask myself if they feel the same at the same time.

Some mothers like me, have someone to help us, others, brave and stoic, do not, and they are my heroes, because I barely make it with these five-month-babies of mine, and that is counting with Aunt Clementina's help. How can some mothers make it without help, and sometimes even with older or younger children? I met some of them at the party, and I bow my head in respect to them, to their enormous capacity of being a multi-tasking human being, without rest, breath nor complaint. And in seeing that garden full of *gemelos* (twins), like a green mantle adorned with identical or very similar kids, I realized that being a mother of twins is a privilege in some way, because not all mothers have the luck to be loved by two at the same time, in similar ways; we are lucky to be seen by two identical faces, to raise two beings at the same time without losing their pace, without losing our minds, gaining time every minute.

May destiny bless us all, and in 20 years, if one of our twins goes to therapy, may it not be because we loved them too much or because we compared them too much to their brother or sister. May in 20 years they re-encounter by chance and, in their conversations, may they realize that their mothers used to take them to these tea parties every year, and then maybe, they had played together in this beautiful garden, in a hot and humid day of summer...

SMILES

This morning something awesome happened. Since the babies wake up too early, we bring them to our bed. They lay on their backs and start their morning session of babbling, as if they were telling us all about what they dreamed last night. In the meantime, David gets ready for work. And the boys laugh so hard and sing and brighten our day which is just starting. But today I noticed that Mauricio was quiet... he was observing his brother carefully. Diego was giving him classes of babbling with little squeals, and cooing mixed with blown raspberries. Mauricio was attentively looking and looking, while Diego was apparently telling him something of utmost importance. When, suddenly, Mauricio smiled at Diego... and Diego smiled back at him! This is the first time I see they smile mutually at each other, in reaction to each other, with total intent. How fantastic to have a sibling of exactly the same age! You might never know loneliness. You will be intimate friends, and will be by each others' side, reacting, reflecting. Today I witnessed a great moment between you. May you always be close, have thousands reasons more to smile at each other, and may nothing separate you as brothers and friends.

"There were more than 20 pairs of twins... What a mix of identical faces, little skirts, and shorts of the same color! That garden was full of mirrors, mobile mirrors, which ran from one place to the next, following one another..."

Chapter 5
Thirty-Six

Today I turned thirty-six. It has been several years since I stopped knowing exactly how old I am, how old I turn. Around when I turned thirty-two it did not matter anymore. The years stopped being important because the reasons why I counted them before (obtain the masters, travel, being a manager, getting married, having a house, having children) had already happened or beginning to happen little by little.

Now I own things: a car, a house, credit cards, stuff. Important things, but non-transcendental, all of them. I have twins, a husband, help, a very extensive and far away family, an uncertain future at work, but very certain at home, friends spaced around the globe who I adore. Those are all transcendental things.

I have never been this fat, or my body so damaged. I still have the stretch marks, my back is crooked, my hip unsynchronized, my fitness is doubtful, my legs have no muscular tone. I have been sleeping no more than three or four hours in a row for a year, with the exception of three nights.

I wake up and go to sleep with two seven-month old babies, one sweet and caramel, the other hurricane and dynamite. One is paused and flirting, the other one restless and in permanent motion. Rodrigo plays and discovers the world gracefully, like showing respect. It fascinates him and he savors every moment, sending me kisses now and then. He seems to sing to his guardian angel in our evening walks. Today, Sebastián learned to sit by himself. David left him on this tummy and when he turned, the baby was sitting up, playing his little piano and looking up at him like saying: "See? I did it by myself, and I am so happy that I am going to play a tune for you!" David was putting up the gates between the kids and the kitchen because Sebastián now reaches unforeseeable corners in the house. This kid of mine is fascinated, discovering new horizons from a completely different perspective; he wants to cover the living room floor, touch the couch from underneath, looks at the coffee table from below, from where he had never seen it before. Rodrigo is learning to sleep better, and wakes up proud of himself; he must feel that his father and I are infinitely thankful for his efforts.

Wherever we go, people stop us several times to tell us how cute the babies are, "Those cheeks, what a smile, how gorgeous." And, three and a half decades after having provoked the same reactions in people, I finally come to understand my mother's pride when she tells me that I was so cute as a baby that people used to stop her in the street. All I want now is to show my kids to the world, put them in a window, have them applauded for how divine they are, the way they illuminate a room when they smile, their growing steps, which seem gigantic to me, increasing, advancing, conquering the world full of toys, milk, hugs, kisses and more kisses...

And to think about what I still have to go! Being a mother of twins is an obsessive work: the bottle, the diaper, the nap, the bottle, the nap, dinner, walk, the bottle, breakfast, the diaper. And so on, forever and ever. And amongst that routine, I am a very entertained woman, that couldn't care less for the health of her marriage, or if the minivan has gas or not, or if my help has time for lunch, or if I called the chiropractor, or if I missed the dentist: all that matters to me are my kids. I would like to buy them clothes every day (almost there), give them new toys (I should stop because we have no more room for them), kiss them all day, all hours, in every space, in each centimeter of their perfect little bodies. I can't remember a thing, nor when I was an aspiring employee and diligent at work, nor when I was a riot in college, nor the party nights celebrating love or un-love, nor when I was an aspiring intellectual who used to walk in the artistic district back in Mexico City.

Of that Sofía, there are only remnants: I talk to my best friends about their work, I read feverishly and religiously, although now I read books on child development, child feeding, child sleeping patterns, anything child-related. Although I was able to read some Vargas Llosa and Allende lately, I focused more on baby-specialized books. Regardless of that, I notice that the more the babies grow, the more I am coming back to be, little by little, the Sofía I was before. I started going to the gym, and I am in talks about my return to work. I listen to my music. I sleep a little bit more. I notice my husband again, who by the way gave me a wonderful card, with thoughts that reflect his relationship with me. It reads: "For my wife from the man who seldom shows it, but who knows that his wife is very smart; who does not often say that she is sweet, but he knows she is; who does not mention that he could not live without her; Happy Birthday my love!"

Signed: Baby, *te quiero mucho, mucho,* you are the best, love, David.
And I cried when he gave me that card because I saw that he was so sincere in his feelings that he filled me with tenderness and then he was carrying Sebastián who was enthusiastically watching his brother, and Rodrigo smiled at me from his crib, and with so much love in that room, how couldn't I be the happiest woman? Clementina, our wonderful help, came in to give me socks, gorgeously wrapped. I opened the other envelope David gave me and it was blue topaz earrings. And those two babies continued smiling, like if they knew it was my birthday. Afterwards, I went to have my hair cut, I tried to make myself pretty (as much as my figure and clothes permitted it) and we went to a 'gym' for babies, where we go every Monday, and good thing David knows all the songs in English which I do not know: the 'Itsy Bitsy Spider', 'If you are happy and you know it clap your hands', 'Patty pat patty pat baker's man', 'Ring around the rosy a pocket full of posies...'

And then I went with Clemen and the babies to get myself something at the mall, and the sweater that I liked but did not fit me, but I bought it anyway because it will someday, and David arrived with my carrot cake, we fed the babies, and took them for their walk. Sebastián was on the backpack, who fell asleep super quickly, with his denim hat covering his eyes, and Rodrigo in the stroller, singing and singing as he was going.

My father told me this morning on the phone the years that I have are reasons for joy because I have everything: family, food on the table, babies who are cherubs, and people who love me. And he is right. Despite the horrendous distance that restrains me from being close to many of my friends and family as much as I want, I am very lucky. *Ajúa!* I hope that my good star does not miss the road. We will keep charging ahead in life, and every day, I fear death less, because I gave life, I created it, doubly, I am not only myself anymore, I exist in these two pieces of flesh who are growing too fast. I can die now, but I will survive in them. And they, in their kids. And so on forever. I turned thirty-six today.

Chapter 6

Visiting during Christmas

We just came back from Salem, Massachusetts. There is where David's aunt lives and we went to visit because she had yet not met our twins, her only grandnephews. Today I decided that these babies of ours are divine and terrible entities, who have to be enjoyed in all their graces. I laughed all day long. Neither Sebastián nor Rodrigo have any idea of what is logical, of what should have an order, or of what is convenient to do. All they care is to be happy, comfortable, and to satiate their curiosity. It does not matter if the standing 2-feet elephant, made of porcelain from China, is a decoration, because sincerely speaking it very well looks like something I can climb on and if possible, lick, Sebastián thought. And there he went crawling, in that house that is nearly a museum with so much adornment, ceramic, tea tables and glass, to see if the elephant made a noise or if the taste was at least good. Of course we stopped him in time, but in that very moment, he discovered a huge Christmas bell, the size of a teapot, hanging from the ceiling, that shined up there like a sun, and my precious baby reached to touch it, he knelt on the floor, opened his arms wide and called him "ta ta ta ta ta", and my heart broke of tenderness and we all smiled. This innocent of mine was calling the bell, because, who knows, maybe the bell wanted to come down and play down here, where the rug is fluffy and blue, where there is a stool that if you stand holding on to it, you see a series of black and white things all in a row, and when grandpa plays them they sound so nice. A piano, of course. I put both babies, one on each of grandpa's legs, while Rodrigo played sensibly but irregularly the black keys of the low tones, and Sebastián hammered the white keys of the high tones. The neighbors must have thought that whoever was playing the piano at Arlene's was pretty drunk.

Then, Sebastián discovered a Santa Claus of porcelain, and ran immediately to it, and grandaunt Arlene, the owner of such a beautiful and decorated house, brought it down to him, put it on the floor, and as if that was not enough, wound up the blessed figurine which my baby watched without blinking for a while, fascinated for the circular movement, the little music that came out of it and that rhythm that was contagious of the sweetness that all music boxes carry eternally. In the meantime, Rodrigo discovered the stairs. Like all typical houses founded and built more than 250 years ago, the stairs are narrow and the steps short, that is to say: they are perfect for an 11-month-old baby, of chubby and strong legs, with enough coordination to leave our mouths wide open while he handled them with skill and precision. Plus, the rail was full of pine boughs and poinsettias, and of holiday golden ornaments, oh my, Rodrigo was climbing the stairs of the years, of the millennium of joy, and just to think what was up there, he even sped up, and his little butt swung quickly, while his little arms reached for the next step and pulled in perfect coordination with his right knee. Silly me, I did not bring the video.

The two affected ones by this whole baby ordeal and baby invasion were two dogs: Taz and Gina. Both were quite grumpy, because of jealousy I'd think, although they behaved very friendly with the babies, licking their ears, sniffing them kindly, and investigating if these things on the floor were two toys, two puppies or twin squirrels. Rodrigo pushed Gina away with his little hand on her jaw, Sebastián fled from them as if they were yucky medicine, but both smiled at them from the distance, because to them, the dogs were also indecipherable.

And those Christmas trees, my goodness, Mom, why don't you put a tree like this in each room of the house like my great-aunt? Sebastián asked me with his eyes. Because this saintly woman --who should dedicate herself to be a professional decorator-- has a Christmas tree in each and every room of the house. When I went to the bathroom I looked twice in case I was sitting on a tree branch. And they are all spectacularly ornamented, I have to mention that each tree had a theme, and she said "well, sure my dear, for example, this one in the kitchen is after The twelve days of Christmas, and there are pears, the partridge, the hen, the five rings, the dove..." Wow, this woman must have tons of boxes which she takes out every year to put the house in such a beautiful state, "yes, she said, it takes me one week to put everything up and two or three to take it down". That is dedication, and yet even the dog had something Christmassy, with a big red bow on the collar.

The centerpiece of the table was a typical New England village, the lake, the figurine skaters, and houses with chimneys. Santa Claus was everywhere: in the ornaments, in the china, in the tablecloth, on the cleaning rags, on the bathroom towels, stuffed and sitting on the chairs, and on the entrance door. Even my pajama which is a gift from her has Santa hundreds of times on it. And my babies, in their glory, in a house with so many new things for their eyes and their imagination, right now they must be dreaming in red, green and golden tones.

Lunch show came, and thanks for portable things, we could sit them in their feeding chairs, they ate their peas, carrots, cereal, apple and as a closing, their cheerios, with which they made everybody laugh because of their funny ability to take them in their little fingers and bring them to their mouths. All this in a typical New England kitchen, all wood, with old signs of stores hanging, and iron bases for hot things on the walls. We had a gorgeous meal of chicken with capers and artichokes, a spectacular beet salad, while Clemen told me that grandaunt Arlene reminded her of her Tía Raquel, who raised her in Mexico City. She was a sophisticated lady with good taste. And while Clemen saw everything with joy and a touch of the past, Arlene's heart filled with this torrent of sweetness that are Sebastián and Rodrigo, that heart which is still in pain after the loss of her (absolutely great) husband Jim.

We almost had to clean Grandpa's drooling of fascination for his only grandsons, his wife was so happy to see all of us together and smiling, David watched that Sebastián did not break any of those antiques that might be worth so much, and I smelled Rodrigo's butt because it was 4 already and he had not pooped. The dogs saw us and participated entwined in our feet, wanting to play with the kids' toys, asking themselves when these two would be leaving so I can be again the center the attention?

Somebody called to ask if Arlene could help them set up for a party, and she very courteously responded she was very busy with her grandnephews, so sorry. For presents, she gave them two rugs in the form of a bee, with a rounded head with antennas, which Rodrigo attacked with kisses the moment they came out of the bag, what a nice and soft thing was the head, plus the little balls in the antennae that I can bite, mommy, what a nice present, look, he told me as he was laying on his belly. And as a surprise, she gave them an electric train, big, beautiful, one of those that really run by themselves. That train she bought for Jim, her gone husband, some years ago, because he liked trains, and that Christmas morning a long time ago, he, and Dave and Dave's father put it together and they had a blast. Later on she put it away, and since he died she had not given out anything that belonged to Jim, and this is the first thing that she does. Of course she never opened it after that day, and now my babies have the honor of inheriting such a beautiful and significant present.

When I had a minute, I went out to walk for five minutes, because that house was like an oven, tremendously hot inside. I don't know if it was because the heat was too high or because there was so much love floating in the air. The first time that we tried to put the twins to nap it was very difficult, because there was so much in those bedrooms that they had never seen before: the yellow wallpaper with blue flowers that coordinated perfectly with the bed cover, and the carpet and the curtains; or the wall full of small paintings and drawings; and that huge window, mommy, with such an enormous tree out there and the way the sun hit it and brought the shadow of the branches to the bed, and the branches moved, mommy, so stop bothering with the bottle, don't even dream that I will nap, don't you see all those stuffed bears above the cabinet? So we tried, but it was impossible, and I thought that it had been a useless effort to bring the port cribs, with the blankets, and their Piggy and Moosey, which they hug when they sleep, so we took them down and in the second try they did nap, they were so exhausted. Or course with my luck, Rodrigo finally fell asleep and I gingerly stood up and when I did, cccrrinncccchhhhhhhh... the floor squeaked as if I weighed three times what I do, with that wood of old houses that has its own amplifiers integrated, so I had to leave little step by little step each time Rodrigo snored, and even then I almost woke him up twice making my way the three feet to the door.

But the most important thing of all was that we made the day for their grandaunt and for grandpa, brother and sister, so in need of love, so proud of their grandsons, who did not tire of admiring them, kissing them, making faces and my babies, the stars, shining, two comets that were hasty because the day was far too short. When we drove back, everything was fine, Sebastián slept, but we had to make a pit stop because Rodrigo did (finally) poo. And then he did fall asleep. But when we drove through Hartford, a city with traffic, lights, trucks, none of which they liked, Sebastián was the first one to be woken up, complain, scream, get grumpy, and of course, wake up his brother. As soon as Rodrigo was up, Sebastián fell asleep again, but with Rodrigo we had to try almost half an hour because he was super angry at the lights, the noise, mommy, what am I doing here and where is my crib, and why do you have me tied to this chair? Poor baby, he cried and cried until he fell asleep. And when he did I thought: oh, my son, we had to come to see this sweet lady who had not met you yet, and who longed for you and who loves you so much, because if you only saw how she looks at you, how she is tender with you, you will grow and you will understand that making an elder person happy is an act of angels, and you are a little angel, my love, sleep peacefully, we are almost home and you will then sleep all comfortable with your Piggy in your crib. I prayed for one of those white witches of Salem to come help me and make them not be awoken again.

When we left Grandpa could not say good bye because tears wouldn't let him. Once more I corroborated how strong are the genes, how much the blood calls, because that man with his seventy-something years, drove eight hundred miles from North Carolina to come and see his grandsons, to see them climb his legs and to make him get on fours and crawl with them. He knows he is infinite in them, because in their lives that start, they renew his. And he knows that his genetic code will survive in Sebastián and Rodrigo, and to feel immortal was what, I think, made him tear up when we left.

Having Twins

Chapter 7

Having twins is to hear the lullaby in echo from the mobiles on top of their cribs when we put them to sleep. It is to prepare double the bottles, because when one sees a bottle, the other one wants it. It is having two car seats and shushing all the time because the other twin is napping. It is two high chairs, two cribs, two identical pairs of little shoes, double the smiles in the morning, two pediatrician bills, booking double-time appointments with the doctor.

Having twins is always having one in your arms and watching the other one, make time to be with one at the time and wondering what to be a mother of a singleton is like. It is going to the supermarket with one baby at the time, alternating them, and when people comment on how cute he is, you need to tell them he is a twin.

Having twins is being fascinated by their differences, marveling by how alike they are, asking yourself how on Earth they manage to hide their little red ball in the most unexpected corners of the house. It is to be the center of attention, the exception, the "oh my, how do you do it?" Having twins is never being alone, each parent with one baby, plus whoever is helping that day, the three of us barely enough to handle these little ones.

Having twins is having two baby monitors turned on in the kitchen while they nap and I write, and watching which one woke up looking at the two monitors, like a tennis match. It is feeding them in their high chairs, while they look at each other like two lovers who have not seen each other in ten years; they stretch their hands to touch each other like in the *callejones* (alleys) in Guanajuato. It is to feel guilty because you are with one and not with the other one, and seeing how one of them crawls to your feet to tell you with his body-language that he also loves you… despite the fact that you are with his brother.

Having twins is to have two peaceful babies, who transform themselves into ferocious enemies if they fight over the toy or the balloon or whatever there is only one of. It is to try to teach them how to give in or share. It means to get them confused in the middle of the night when they cry and you go in the wrong room, so you wake up the one who was asleep and the one who was crying to start with is crying louder because, well, why are you taking so long?

Having twins is not only having problems and joys by the double, but multiplied exponentially, the good and the bad. And when you fall asleep, you sleep so deeply because you are tired for two, and when you play with them, you play until you succumb to exhaustion because you are playing with two, and when you cry of happiness because you see one of them do something for the first time, your heart almost explodes within because it was not designed to host the happiness of two hearts. So everything in your life expands, nothing contracts, except your sleeping hours, the waking hours now stretch so you can do more, the washing machine washes and washes all day, the bottles are a continuum that flows from the babies' lips to the sink to the drying to the filling to the babies' lips again. All day. All night.

Having twins means two shots instead of one, it is to listen them cry inconsolably in unison, it is to want to rip their pain out, and to give up because it is impossible.

Having twins is to want to have another baby, and one more, because if the ones to come are as cute as the ones you already have, there would be no reason not to have more. Right.

Having twins is wondering how the heck do mothers of triplets do this?

"Having twins is wondering how do mothers of triplets to this?"

Has Anyone Seen My Babies?

Chapter 8

Last Thursday, Sebastián started climbing on the dinner table chairs. With his typical intrepidness, he held on with one little hand to the edge of the table, the other one on the back of the chair, lifted the small foot as high as he can until his knee helped him get on top completely and there! He sat on the chair, which now lasts three seconds because yesterday he started to stand on the chairs too. His twin brother (how could he stay behind?) tried it too and defined a different style: mounting by his belly. First he put his belly on the chair, with two hands stretched out like rubber until he reached the other side, held his feet up, kicked and kicked in the air while he pushed himself until he could kneel and sit down on the chair with bright smile on his face. I watched them with the fearsome amazement with which you watch the tightrope walker march 120 feet above ground with no safety net below. My heart diminishes three sizes when they do their juggling acts.

They also started climbing on top of the center table. We try telling them no, which is completely useless. We better cushion their falls, because they have no intention of listening yet. Today I sat on the floor on the back of the couch, and they decided to find me not by foot, but by air! They climbed on the couch, jumped on the back of it and tried to descend on the other side as if they were professionals climbing K2. I thought, "I am glad I am here to catch them. If not, the bruises could have been considerable." The same with the rocking chair; they use it as a boat and balance it as if the storm were thick and the waves high. Now their growing bodies allow them to do bigger things: escalate, get up, climb, reach high, see from another perspective, reach where it was impossible before. Their instinct to put their knees up is superior. They cannot stop; they must discover. They must get atop.

And I ask myself: has anybody seen my twin babies? They were two little guys who were just crawling in the living room. Little balls of skin and sweetness, they followed each other like a little train, stopping here and there to play with the mini turtle or baby hippo. They gurgled, smiled, and slept three times a day, more than an hour each time. One was fluffy and sat like the gymnasts: open legs and straight back. The other one crawled commando style: first the elbow, then the left hand. That is how they used to entangle themselves between my legs. My babies did not open doors, did not run, did not fall, did not have boo-boos, did not get into the fridge, did not fight nor did they ever bit each other. They were two *tamalitos* of sugar, that although did not sleep through the night, their little heads were free of bruises and their soft lips never bled because they hit the edge of the bathroom door while tripping. Has somebody seen them? Because someone has tried to substitute them with two audacious explorers, disguised as small children, who inhabit my house and turn it upside down. The toys are everywhere, they speak a foreign language which I am yet to find which part of the Earth it's from.

Sometimes they adore me and sometimes I am clearly on their way to reach their goal in their most important expedition. They spread avocado on me, they step on me, the jump on my back as if I were a buoy, they laugh when I tickle them but these little boys demand I do not stop, and my babies only demanded the bottle. These toddlers that are here in my house, I must accept, look a lot like my babies, but it cannot be that they have grown so fast. It is impossible. Just a few days ago Sebastián crawled for the first time at the beach, and Rodrigo stood up holding on to the couch. Now this couch is one more step for these boys that I have in the house, it is one more place where to jump hard and possibly hurt themselves badly. I watch them in wonder because of their new capabilities, their aberrant incapacity to understand "No," their eyes open wide trying to understand how this world functions. I can almost see their brains grow moment by moment, with their eyes catching every small detail: the gestures, the attitudes, the ways to hold things.

Today I was blowing some balloons for them and I saw them holding the un-inflated balloons, put them to their mouths and expelling air from their mouths. They were imitating me, like saying "Mommy, teach me, tell me how you make this flaccid thing become a magic colorful ball that floats in the air." They look inside everything, everything that has a little hole they peek in; maybe they will discover something fun and preferably new. They die to watch through the window because if something is happening out there, they must know. Before, my babies were happy in my arms with my songs and my breast. These two substitutes announce a future of rowdy play and maybe a short visit to the emergency room. They also tell me that they are on their way to develop fully as little boys, bunches of energy and that all I have to do is provide care, certainty, love and lots of patience. That is why I am asking: Has anybody seen my babies?

Homemade Dwarves

Chapter 9

We have a little dwarf in the house. He goes silently by the aisles, and suddenly appears between the furniture. As an only sign he has his smile and his blind decision to continue walking. He is small, hardly reaches the middle of my thigh, has short hair, and feet like Charles Chaplin. He navigates with two little invisible antlers which indicate to him where his twin brother is hiding, where the cap of the body lotion is and where the last cheerio of this morning fell. He does not talk, does not yell, does not fuss, but just walks in a hurry, like groping in the dark, calculating how to avoid falling down. This little dwarf does not want me to intercept him because in his mind he always has clarity about where he wants to go and what he wants to achieve.

Sometimes we interfere between him and his goal. But sometimes he gets tired, he stumbles, falls as if the best football players had trained him: on his side and rolling over his shoulder not to hurt himself, and he lays belly up, like he had forgotten where he was going, and looks to the ceiling and starts to drum on the floor with his heels, telling the floor that he is on his way, give him one minute, he is just taking a brief break because this business of walking is so tiring. At the same time, he sings. *"Tatatatatata... Tatata tataa... mamama... tatataaa... Mamaa..."* That is when I get close to him. I kiss his belly and tickle him on his sides and he laughs wholly, and between the smiles he reveals to me his new teeth. There, laying down, he looks like the little baby he was until two months ago, but he is no longer that, he is Mr. Owner of the World, straight, his forehead up, a wide smile, who goes from the kitchen to the bathroom without asking for permission. He is the owner of this house, of this Earth, and has a tremendous responsibility of inspiring his brother to walk, that twin brother who today took four steps in a row and shortly will become the second gnome in the house, to enchant it with their steps which exude star dust wherever they walk.

There are butterflies over their heads, and an iridescent light that is created when the air through which they cross opens to let them through. They are angels, goblins, little beings that inflate my heart of pride and remind me of how wonderful the human body and mind are, so little and so great at the same time. They go by this life decided, their muscles fortifying their future, with their eyes on the toy, the food, the sippy cup, and tomorrow on their dreams, on their loved one, on the horizon.

But for now there is magic surrounding the house, as if fairy tales were real, and their main character were this little one, who goes around all the house with his little feet, which take him from here to there untiringly, reminding us that the sweetness in life is the road, not the finish line.

"He is the owner of this
house, of this Earth,
and has a tremendous
responsibility of inspiring
his brother to walk, that
twin brother who today took
four steps in a row
and shortly will become
the second gnome
in the house…"

Chapter 10
Do You Remember?

Mom,

Today in the morning, while the babies slept, I remembered that it was a year ago that neither they nor I used to sleep in this house. I recall the weather outside made no difference: cold, sun or snow, we didn't even know. We had two newborns in the house. Two little ones, small creatures of sand and velvet, wrapped in a halo of tulle, a supernatural pair that broke all the paradigms of having a first-born only once in your life. David and I had two first-borns... In one single moment in our lives.

You arrived at the hospital looking good, with a blue sweater that looked great on you, your pin that matched your earrings, your impeccable hair, your eternal good smelling perfume. You entered like a blizzard of maternity into that room, like all grandmas who come to see their grandchildren, filled with anxiety, emotion, ingenuity, thankfulness to life which is letting them see the sprouts of their sprouts, their genes mixed with other genes in a completely new being. In two beings, in our case. All the headaches that you had because of me, I paid them back to you that day, when I made you a grandmother. When in that generational staircase, you moved one step up, and me another one, and my grandma another one. Because I was made a mom like you, and then you became what my grandmother was for me, but now for my kids. And in that chain of blood and feminine energy, we interlaced once more, and tied two new beings that came to regenerate us, to recommence our lives.

When I saw you enter, I knew that my children were most fortunate to have you as a grandmother, so intelligent and tenacious, so alive and enterprising. You held them, I imagine, with the same sweet face you held me for the first time. Giving birth is to be born again, and I was reborn that day, and so were you. You knitted little hats while you were in the hospital, while I half slept between the intravenous saline and the painkillers, how awful were those days. My body was waving good-bye to a terribly difficult pregnancy, with a horrible recovery, with air bloated in my intestines, contractions bringing my uterus back to normal, a continuous pain of 12 centimeters of stitches, with my breasts swollen and sensitive, organs inflamed, and at the same time, with the enormous joy of seeing Sebastián and Rodrigo complete, healthy, divine. What a contradiction. And at the same time that I suffered, I boasted for the luck of being a mother. I would never do it again, but I would not change it for anything. Then we had to go back home, that nest we have been cushioning for months, Dave and I, and that now could warmly receive babies and grandma. And just then, the real adventure started...

Do you remember we were in pajamas all day long? I did not take them off. I just changed them for clean ones because I was in them for weeks, for months, those pregnancy pajamas that had the split openings in the front to breast feed. You washed them for me, you washed everything for me, "Let me hold on because she will wash me too," my grandma used to say when you used to start ravaging around the house picking up clothes and things to wash. We took showers... sometimes... "If they let us" like we used to sing when we made plans: "as soon as the babies sleep, I will make the soup" you used to say. "I will take a shower" I said. "I will call your father." "I will check my e-mail." And while I finished giving them the breast, you gave them the bottle to supplement, and change their diapers. You then started singing that romantic old Mexican song, changing the lyrics to make me laugh: *"Si nos dejan, nos vamos a querer toda la vida...si nos dejan, nos vamos a bañar en este día..."* (If they let us, we will love each other all our lives, if they let us, we will take a shower today...). You made me laugh so much with your singing improvisations! And boy, did we need a good sense of humor to survive the task of feeding two babies every three hours, which took us two hours each. We had an hour between feedings, sometimes we did not even have time to go to the bathroom, when we turned: "wahh wwaaahhh wahhh" they were already awake again and hungry! And that was twenty-four hours, all day, no breaks, there was no truce nor rest. I remember that as soon as I put my head on the pillow, I closed my eyes and immediately I heard one of the babies crying, and I did not want to open my eyes, but I had no choice.

Those babies had to eat and I was the provider. My breasts were enormous, heavy. Sebastián emptied them especially at an exorbitant speed. Glug glug glug, three, four minutes, ciao, there, my breast was empty, he was satisfied, asleep in my arms, that little baby of dark eyes and fishy mouth. There were some nights we used to fall asleep together, me in the rocking chair, he in my arms, on the boppy pillow. Dawn came and found us often together, me exhausted, and him very hungry and wet. He always latched well, since he was very little.

Rodrigo was a completely different story: he was so impatient that he raged because the milk was not in his mouth immediately, in the very moment he wanted it. Latching and feeding was quite complicated.

That concert of the body of the mother with the baby's, in a survival act to stay alive will always leave me astonished. How wise of Mother Nature, that instead of making a new human to depend on something foreign to her, gave the mother herself the wonderful task of creating the sustenance within her body, and of being the provider not only of nutrients, but of warmth, caress, dedication; because all of those things happen with breast feeding. It is a giving of ourselves to another person, defying fatigue and going crazy with love when you have that being, surged from yourself, fastened to your person, physically and emotionally, like a continuous entity, not even continuous, but one in all. That is, I have no doubt, the base of all emotional relationship in the future.

Remember the cradle? These little angels used to fit in one. One on the side of the other one, one facing east, the other one west, wearing the things you knit them, wrapped in the piqué blankies that you brought them, like little *tamalitos*. Rodrigo always put his hand out, like he was singing *La Vida Loca,* remember how much he made you laugh when finally you wrapped him perfectly well, made a little bundle, you deposited him in the cradle and immediately he started whirling until he freed his hands? And the day that I hung the small stuffed animals on the side of the cradle, remember how he stared at that little bear? Remember that, Mom? His eyes, open wide, that bear had him startled.

The other one who was startled was his father with so much liquid that came out from their peepees and ended up on us, on the changing table, on the wall. How many times we got all wet, our clothes, our hands, even our faces! Endless diaper changings. Wailing babies, hated to be undressed. David called the changing table the torture chamber. And one of his many chores was emptying the diaper receptacles. You used to say he looked like a tired Santa carrying all those piles of sausage-linked dirty diapers on his shoulders out of the rooms every other day.

You used to send me to bed after the feedings, begging me to rest. Meanwhile, you rocked them to sleep, then went to the kitchen and cooked something tiptoeing and trying to make the least noise not to wake anyone up. You took the clothes out of the drier, you folded them, you prepared the formula, you washed bottles and the hundreds of little plastic items of the breast pump. You got everything ready for the next feeding which often started as soon as you were done. You prepared me this special Mexican drink that is good for new mothers, *atole,* made of cornstarch and milk. Until we realized that milk was not helping the digestion of the babies, so you did it with water. You kept cooking me things that were good for me and not bad for them, I remember sometimes I was feeding one of the babies, and you were sitting by me feeding me a delicious sandwich because I was starving and had no time to sit and eat. You always filled my water bottle; I went through so much water! But you quenched my thirst, not only for liquid, but for maternal care also. To this day, I do not know how I would have done it without you.

David came back from work, and then you took a break, finally. You and him alternated nights to stay with me and the babies. I remember one night I heard Sebastián crying, and I came in their room, and there you were, trying to bottle feed them both at the same time, because you did not want to wake me up, I had just recovered from a fever and had not slept at all in 24 hours, because the babies were very colicky. Your face full of grief and frustration, the babies crying, my grogginess, Mom, you were trying so hard to please everybody. And you did.

Some evenings were lethal, remember? Between five and eight the babies were super fussy, we were going out of our minds with the two of them crying like crazy. I used to read trying to find answers, ways of doing things better, despite the tens of books that I read before delivery, this was the real test, I had no idea it would be so hard. Not to mention my hormones, on a joy ride, on a roller coaster, I cried so easily, I was so tired, so sensitive, so damn happy. And you were there to help me release all those feelings. David was my pillar, you were my pillow.

Presents used to come to our door everyday. How to keep track of them, open them, enjoy that moment when the wrapping paper gives in and something sweet and useful comes out. These babies got so much stuff, and there you were, ready to wash the new clothes, put the precious teddy bear in the perfect place, sew the hands of the onesies so that the babies would stop cutting themselves with their thin sharp nails.

We had our moments of truth also, you and I, strong characters, wills and different views on many things. We fought, we tensed, but most of the times, we kept quiet and kept moving along. Sebastián and Rodrigo being first in our minds and actions, nothing less but their well being was our first priority.

Remember when we had no idea what was going on in the world? I felt so far away from everything, from everybody. I was isolated here, on an island of pacifiers, wipes, bags under the eyes, rocking chairs and calls to the lactation consultant. I did not watch the news ever. If a war had started in some far away country, I had no idea. If some huge catastrophe had happened, I guess I did not care in those months. You were so nice and filled me up with some basic news now and then. On your "nights off" you were able to watch the news or talk to my Dad back in Mexico.

After a couple of weeks, Dave had to go back to work, and then you had to do the grocery shopping, poor Mom, so used to the warm weather in our country, and now having to deal with snow, ice, heavy jackets, frozen windshields! And when finally I went one day, I called three times, until you told me: if you call again, you will wake them up, now hurry, get it done and come back. OK Mom.

One day I remember I heard you talking by yourself in the kitchen. I had gone to bed to rest, since the night had been horrific, and I recall thinking while still groggy from waking up: "Who is Mom talking with? What is she cutting on the board? Did someone come to visit?" And so I got up, dragged myself to the kitchen, but stopped before getting there, the scene being so endearing: you had Sebastián and Rodrigo on the bouncy chairs at your feet, you were sitting by the kitchen table cutting carrots for the rice, one foot on one bouncy chair, one on the other one, rocking them alternatively, and at the same time, you were telling them the story of Father Wind, the same one you used to tell me when I was little. The babies looking up fascinated by you, mesmerized by your rhythm with your hands and with your feet, and with your fluent words in Spanish. I felt so happy then, so proud of being your daughter, Mom. Do you think Sebastián and Rodrigo will remember that moment? I know I always will. *Gracias. Feliz Día de las Madres.* Happy Mother's Day.

Chapter 11
Toddler Twins

A toddler is a grown-up man inside the body of a baby. He wants to say so much, yet his mouth can only utter certain sounds; that is frustrating at times, but it gives him the ability to learn a new word every day, which is actually fascinating. He wants to climb heights that are impossible for him. He wants to give his opinion and can only utter certain sounds.

A toddler is a little boy with the soul of a great wise man, his logic is perfect, his amazement in front of adult reasoning, embarrassing. Time has no way of being measured in a toddler mind: tomorrow, later, five minutes, they are all useless phrases, empty meanings; on the contrary, "now" is completely understandable, quite easy for him to grasp and often impossible to meet.

Toddlers have two roles in the kitchen: they are the chefs and direct the cooking from the counter, but when it comes to eating they are the pickiest of all. One day they only eat carbs and half a bag of cheerios is gone, another day they decide ham is in order and pack on protein like there will be no more meat in the world tomorrow. Bananas are good and if they don't finish their half, they can always smear it on the floor or on the table or on the brother's head.

Twin toddlers pose the surmounting challenge of all those qualities in a scale not twice as difficult, but oftentimes ten times more difficult. If one brother does not find the answer "no" acceptable, the other one never will either. If one toddler cries, his twin also gets upset, although sometimes he is the best one to cheer the brother in disgrace up. Disgrace in this case could be that the brother did not get a third lollypop, or that he was told not to put the phone in the tub or maybe when trying to type on mommy's laptop with his hands full of peanut butter, he got reprimanded.

The way toddler twins feel for each other certainly gives the human race an example of loyalty and tenderness. I have seen Sebastián bring Rodrigo his adored Piggy when he is crying at his fullest, and even though Piggy just comes to serve as a tissue, I know he appreciates the gesture. And when Sebastián swims like a madman at the Y, splashing his surroundings in a way that only Keiko can, Rodrigo tries to follow him since it looks like so much fun. I will never forget Sebastián patting Rodrigo´s head at the airport on a late flight arrival, Rodrigo being miserably tired and Sebastián trying to console him with what he had best at hand: his love for him. They learn from each other, from trying a different food to drawing and smashing playdough. It is always fun to see them grow together but into individuals that could not be more different.

When you have toddler twins, unexpected things happen. Last night, as I was changing into my pajamas, I took off my shirt and dust of white powder flew around - debris from a battle of talc in the morning, which I lost against these two contenders, who were determined to blanket me in white. They found it so enticing to run after me, talc on hand. Then, while putting on my pajamas, I notice there are stickers on the wall – grapes and cars. Apparently one of my twins has interior design tendencies. I leave my bedroom and go to say night-night while David is reading them a book, and Rodrigo says: "Mami, come, I want to give you a big hug" and after he gave it to me he says "that was a big hug mami". And it was. Sebastián gives me a super kiss, one of those that leave you dizzy with elation and saliva, and both get belly down on the floor to keep listening to the story while looking at the colorful images of the book. These days, books fill up this house with fantasy. There are nannies who take their grandsons to dance with the zoo animals. Eggs which grow so much and dinosaurs pop out. Frogs who like to trot and not leap, learning to go around as they like, not as anyone expects them to. There are girls who take care of reindeers and train them how to fly. The world is a nebulous place between reality and imagination when you have toddlers in your house.

Having toddler twins is also a matter of getting good at answering questions. Sebastián and Rodrigo are marveled by new things. Why is the little hand of the clock slower than the long hand? Why is the snow melting into water? Why does the mirror reflect a spot of light on the wall?

Toddler twins can also serve as a good example of war tactics. I am sure many a battle expert could come to this house and learn a lot about combat strategies, ways to hurt the enemy and get what he wants no matter what it takes: conciliatory skills, trading, convincing, calling for a third party as a consultant (normally mommy) or making the enemy bleed via a good bite or leaving a good mark (a red and purple bruise usually). I remember reading about how some entities in Nature live thanks to another entity. They depend on each other for life. Some birds live on hippos' backs. Some fish swim and live around certain types of whales. They do things for each other: one cleans and helps maintain health, the other one provides food or energy. They are bound for life together. Could this be the same case in twins? I cannot imagine their lives apart, now that they bounce and sing and often decide for themselves, I see them interact and wonder what their lives would be if separated. I think they would be different little persons. The way they are intermingled together is amazing, how they know each other often even better than I do, how they flow from the rhythm of one to the rhythm to the other, Sebastián sometimes leads the fast and energetic playtime and then gets wound down when his brother decides to sit down and "read" a book full of fun pictures and colorful trucks.

Toddler twins are like those lion cubs you see in the National Geographic documentaries. They are wild, full of expressions and relentless at play. They know no boundaries, the lioness has to be on the watch 24x7, because the little ones know no fear, they love risk and think they own the jungle. Having a toddler in the house is a joy, an adventure and a lot of cleaning up. Now multiply that by ten, and you have twin toddlers. In this jungle, at 8 at night, the two cubs go to their cribs and dream of backhoes and puppies. The lion and the lioness rest in front of the TV, demolished and satisfied, and fall asleep way before the news come on. Everyone exhausted, happy to hear the silence of the house, the silence of a dormant jungle.

Chapter 12
My Fantasy House

I wonder how a house with one single, not two, toddler is like. I have this glorified image of a place where there is no fighting, there is no need to say the same thing twice, where getting ready to leave the house is not a complete ordeal.

I am probably wrong, but I do know that somewhere in this world the perfect house for toddler twins exist. It would have two of each toy, two identical toys always. The favorite stuffed animals or blankets, those without which nap or sleep time are impossible, would have an integrated chip to locate them anywhere in the house with a remote control. It would also have minute TV cameras in each room that transmit to a portable camera that the mother carries. That way, I could have avoided the Picassos on the wall downstairs, the wonderful hair that Sebastián painted on the rocking cow with a permanent marker and the unexplainable number of quarters that ended up inside the CD player in the minivan.

My fantasy house would have a room just for bouncing and jumping and climbing. It would have cushioned walls, lots of pillows; ladders to climb and spring boards that would let them go wild and preserve their natural monkey instincts intact.

Meals would be served in a room with a removable floor, so when the meal is done, with a push of one button, all the crumbs, pieces of apple and smashed spaghetti would disappear, and a brand clean floor would be laid out.

This ideal house would provide the mother with a special remote control, which she could activate anytime to bring on a distraction or an entertainment in excruciating times. For example, when I am trying to get them dressed. If only I could push a button and some kind of puppet could fall from the ceiling and start dancing or something, while I put pull-ups and shorts and T-shirts on, that would be of so much help, for me and for my mental health, since getting them dressed takes more energy than I could have ever imagined, between the chasing, the convincing (no, we cannot wear winter boots today, it is 80 outside my darrrrrrling), the final battle (me using my two hands to dress, my two legs to pin them down), and the victory (yeah! it only took 20 minutes today!).

An ideal house for toddler twins would have a fridge that has instant, homemade, nutritious meals every day. There would be the "favorites" section, presenting pasta, cereal, cookies, ketchup, avocado; there would be a "must have" section, with proteins, vegetables, and fruit. And the resulting meals would have some of each section, which seems to be the only way to keep everyone happy.

An ideal house for toddlers would have a live-in person with paranormal powers, one of those people who can transmit thoughts without words. Sometimes that is the only way I think these two would understand me. My words sometimes mean absolutely nothing to them, they do not even look at me when I am talking to them, telling them to stop dismantling the train tracks for the third time today, to stop trying to climb the fence that gates the pool, to pick up the trail of cars that they leave as they walk from room to room, or that it is time to nap. Apparently it must be something that only a person with telepathic powers can communicate to them.

In such a house, the TV would actually work only one hour a day. Period. It would probably have to be a TV with batteries that only last that long. That way, even if they wanted to watch another dvd, the TV would not work anyway, so there would be no way to make it work until the next day. Just like when their toys that use batteries run out of juice, they would have to understand that the TV also has limited battery time. I wonder if that would actually work.

In this house, we would have pets that do not require maintenance, they would be mostly self-sufficient. Dogs that walk themselves and don't go off the instant the door is half-inch opened, cats that do not shed and fish that eat off from each other and then regenerate. Entertainment for our twins would still be there, without the feeling that we have a third child to take care of in the house.

A house for twin toddlers would have a single bedroom with a slide door in the middle, that is soundproof, childproof, and if possible, twin-proof. So when Rodrigo wakes up at 2 am, this door will defend his brother from his wailing, but when they want to be together, they could actually share a room.

How about a kitchen for toddler twins that had a separate mini-kitchen in it, like a replica of ours, but to their size? It would have cabinets, and the same utensils and pots and plates, but to their size. The plastic kitchenette they have is not really cutting it anymore, since now they want to use spices and they want to toss pasta and use the whisk, or better, press the buttons on the blender and hold the mixer. In this ideal house, they would have all these, fit to their little hands and with all the safety they need.

There would be a room just dedicated to art in this house. Walls and floors that could be painted, drawn on and scratched. Washable paints, thick brushes, thin brushes, containers to paint on, crafts to enjoy, Telemann in the background, mixed with some Raffi, Mozart and soft salsa. This room would have a wonderful attachment: a cleaning robot! One that at the end of the imaginative session, would come out of the closet, hand out a bin for Sebastián and Rodrigo to put their colorfully-stained clothes in, and when they were out of the room, it would dispose of anything not worth mailing to grandma or putting in their "when I was little" special bin, leaving the room spotless for the next creative day of art.

Most importantly, I am thinking, this house would come equipped with not the normal, frazzled, overtired mom that all houses I know have. This fantasy house would actually have three moms.

'Mom Number One' would be dedicated to enjoy her twins. She would spend all the time she wanted with them, read all those books, sit and enjoy watching the fireflies at night, teach them discipline and kiss them all over when she felt like it. This Mom would come with two servings of patience, since it is important not to loose it when one of the twins climbs out of the crib for the first time or when the other wants you to sing with him London Bridge for the 20th time that day.

'Mom Number Two' would be dedicated to the house itself, but since this fantasy house is pretty easy to maintain, she would dedicate herself to make improvements, paint rooms, decorate, change styles, garden without interruptions and actually go shopping at leisure, without two chimpanzees trying to run out of her sight in the store or whine or refuse to give up the little wooden cart to the cashier so she can scan it. This mom would also be in charge of being an exemplary wife, one that actually showers everyday, has time for pedicures and finds time to romance with her husband.

'Mom Number Three' could go to work, be a professional, think together with other adults, be aware of what happens in the world, have justified opinions on public matters and read her favorite books on the weekends.

And there you have it... Doesn't it sound great? It is so cool to dream...

"... a place where there is no fighting, there is no need to say the same thing twice, where getting ready to leave the house is not a complete ordeal."

Chapter 13

Bye-Bye Babies

They took the cribs yesterday. We sold them really cheap to a Mexican mother who is having twins in February and who does not have a lot of money. She came with her husband, an uncle and a cousin to pick them up. I related to their ability to make of a trip a travel event. It was raining outside when we were waiting for them to come, and while I was taking off the padding and the skirt in Rodrigo's crib, I started crying.

These were the last pieces of furniture that we had which were from the time when they were babies. We are not having more kids, so we would not need them anymore, plus they were taking all that space. I can write a list of twenty reasons why we sold them, but my heart did not want to hear one of them. It sunk the moment I realized that the piece of space and wood and shelter where my little ones had slept when they were barely some weeks old, where they had cooed and learned to stand and smiled in the mornings, was being taken away from me. First they slept in a cradle, one with the head north, one with the head south, but after that they grew and they did not fit. It seems like that is the story of babies, first you hold them in your belly until they have to come out because your belly is not roomy enough and you feel like you are going to explode. Next you put them in a bassinet where they are still entangled in each other's warmth until they start kicking each other and there is no more room so off they go to the crib. When one crib is not enough, you put them in separate cribs, then they move to beds, and I am sure that when they go off to college it is because their minds and bodies don't fit anymore in this house, like Alice in Wonderland when she takes the "make me big" pill and her arms and feet come out of doors and windows of the house, and her head sticks out from the chimney.

They say there are two things you must give your kids: roots and wings. I feel that while we are doing the "root" work, they are already growing their wings, The wings are expanding on their backs and want to fly now and not later, so they say "Bastián is big boy" or "Rigo no need help, *Mami*, myseffff." Separating is such a joy for them and for us sometimes too, except when nostalgia hits and I find myself crying over the things that will never happen again. I will never sit in a dim-lighted room, at two in the morning, watching two little beings bundled up with each other, sleeping a peaceful sleep only babies can sleep. Listening to them breathing, with my chin on the rail, was the softest most beautiful sound I had ever heard.

I will never see daybreak, magnificently orange pulling up the gray blanket of dawn from the window, while Rodrigo is breastfeeding noisily and Sebastián is cooing from the crib. I will never drag myself to that room one more time, the thousandth time it seemed, to change the thousandth diaper, and then when I put them back on their cribs to see them giggle and smile at me and suddenly not feeling exhausted, I was a mother of twins who sometimes wondered if her heart could hold so much love and joy. Those cribs that they took away could tell a whole story of these two first years, they were the silent witnesses of play time, nap time, and night time. They were scrubbed of projectile vomit. They were moved when the pacifier was nowhere to be found. They were pushed when Rodrigo learned that if he leaned enough and with all his strength, he could move the crib a couple inches to the left. They heard the screams when we decided no more bottles.

It was on those cribs where they grew and where I became a mother, a comforter, an actor in a movie for which no one had given me the script, yet we were filming live. There are dozens of pictures of them in their cribs. When they first started sitting up, when they were able to hold their bottles, when one night Sebastián stood up for the first time in his life holding on to the bars. When Rodrigo was asleep, his butt up, snoring away. It was those same cribs which Rodrigo learned to climb out of one day when he decided he was not going to nap. He did it gracefully and without hurting himself, but absolutely determined to let me know that there was no way he was going to sleep that afternoon. So he stayed up and he had a horrific afternoon, being so tired. "Rigo gouchy, *Mami*" as Sebastián described him later. Then there was one day when Rodrigo would not sleep in the crib at all, after our beach vacation, it seemed like a jail to him, and so very reluctantly we went to buy mattresses and beds and now they are "big boys" who sleep on "big boy" beds. Well, let me correct: Sebastián, who is the one who had no problem with his crib, sleeps in his bed all night long. Rodrigo, on the other hand, the instigator to get rid of them, sleeps between David and me every night; he is like a little night dwarf who comes around 5 AM for a little visit and ends up staying over. They look so tiny in the twin size beds, just like they looked when they were two months old and we laid them down on the crib. Bye-bye crib, hello bed. Bye-bye babies. *Mami* will cry a little as daddy pulls your cribs apart, but then life will go on and maybe sometime I will get used to the idea that I don't have babies anymore. Maybe.

Chapter 14: She is Having Twins

My friend Ann is going to have twins. The news was broken to them late October, when Ann had some bleeding and they had to do an ultrasound. Just like me. The bleeding was nothing to worry about; the two beating hearts in the monitor, well, say hello to your new double cargo! Ann is actually a twin herself, but still the twinshock hit hard.

– How long were you in shock, Sofi?
– Mmmmh... A couple of months actually, I don't think the fact that we were having twins sank until after the fourth month (when the unbelievable fear of losing them, since we had lost a baby just before, stopped making my heart skip beats day and night, I did not say).

I love Ann, she is one of my best friends, I think we are close because we are both from another country and in love with two New Englanders who continue to amaze us as husbands.

"Wait until you see your Dave as a father, Ann, I told her one day on what now has become our bi-weekly call, "when you see him holding those two babies tenderly, when he blows raspberries to them, when he passes them on to you after bathing them. Get ready, you are going to fall in love all over again with him." I can only see her nod when I tell her this, but she will never know what I mean until it actually happens to her, like all the other things. Shall I tell her that yes, this will be the most exhilarating experience of her life, and also the most tiring and trying?

Shall I share with her the fact that one day she will feel doubly blessed for having two babies at a time, and the next she will cry in agony because both of them are screaming at the same time and she cannot soothe and carry them both at the same time? Shall I tell her that her life in the first months will be a blur, a fog, she will operate by instincts, shower if there is time, wear breast feeding shirts like her second skin, forget to call people back, curse the mail carrier for being noisy and waking up the babies, eat half and cold meals, call the pediatrician and hang up feeling he did not understand her level of concern with constipation? The division of night and day will be merely artificial, her nipples will be sore, she might get engorged, shall I tell her about mastitis? No, no, that would scare her too much. Let her concentrate on enjoying her double pregnancy.

– "Sofi, I feel I have no energy for anything... when did you stop feeling tired all day?" (To this day, that is how I feel, I do not mention)
– "Let's see, I was actually tired most of my pregnancy, but that is probably because I was sick every minute of it, dehydrated seriously twice, but your pregnancy seems to be going so much better than mine, Ann. I do remember in the seventh month I was more lively and active (of course, by then I was so huge I could barely move the mammoth I had become, I do not point out).

Should I warn her about stomach viruses and the effect it has on a house with twins? One gets the virus one week, the other the next, so you pretty much run the washer all day for three weeks, milk and doubtful liquids coming out of all places. I better not; with some luck, she will not have to go through that. I better share with her our experience with the amnio (the procedure recommended for mothers-to-be who are over 35, by which they take amniotic fluid out of the sac and run tests). I think that might come handier now, and how we decided against it when they told us there was always the risk to penetrate the same sack twice - a membrane that was not exactly designed by Nature to be punctured.

Diapers, that is another thing I might share with her now, she should start buying them, saving coupons, creating a stack in a closet that will make you think you have too many until you finish up all those boxes, your husband has carried them all out, and you look at these two bundles in the crib, less than 10 pounds each, and think "Wow, for two cute little guys they do pooh and pee a lot!"

I sent her the information about the Mothers of Multiples club in her area, but she did not sound that interested. I did not either, when I was pregnant; it was not until Sebastián and Rodrigo were two months old that I was able to come to a meeting and I met some of the most extraordinary women in my life. I saw them all in that room, gathered in a council of double-motherhood, talking about all these things while my brain (or the few neurons that were still working at the time) realized: they have all gone through what I am going through, and they made it. Look at them, some of them even had time to blow dry their hair and put on mascara! I can do it, I can make it, they have, I will. And I did. And having survived that first year made me feel like the most achieved woman on earth, like a warrior who won the battle, like those alpine hikers that you see on TV when they step on the very top of Mount Everest. Ann will have that feeling too, I am sure. She will go through the test, she will get through, with the help of all of us, because now I know that I would have never ever made it without my mother, my sister, Clemen, Janet, David of course, the long list of friends who gave us their support, and my new clan at MOM's (Mothers of Multiples). They knew what I was talking about. They gave me proven solutions to problems that only arise with twins, and it was a sisterhood that I will always be in debt with.

Shall I tell Ann that she should cancel her subscription to the New York Times? Or shall I wait to do that for her after the twins are born, and the stack grows every day, news of the world piling up at the door, sending a clear message to the outside: "we are breast feeding baby twins in this house, we have time for nothing else, please do not disturb." Maybe I will wait for that on too.

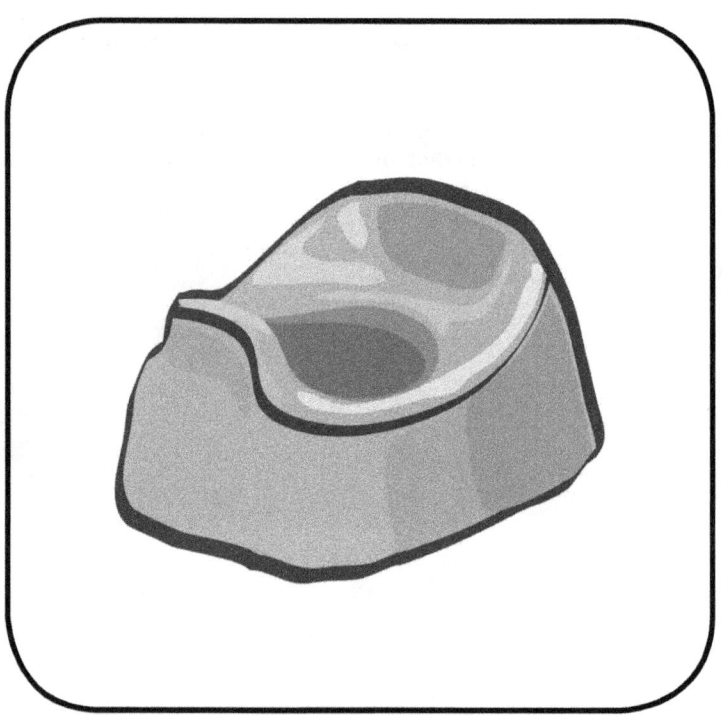

Chapter 15
La Bacinica (Or On Potty Training)

Some books say there is no such thing as "potty training." They say the kid will stop wearing diapers when he or she is ready. As often happens, the authors of those books obviously did not have twins. In our case, this potty training experience has been more like a "let's see what my brother does" kind of process.

Last year, when they were two, we got them a potty chair, one of those that sits on the floor and can be used as a stool later on when they are completely potty trained. One of those products which are successful because they sell: a) A solution to a current problem and b) The dream of a future without such problem. Smart marketing. Terrible liars. The potty chair was brought in the bathroom, and of course, being a single item in the house, turned out to be a reason for quarrel: "I want to go!" "No, I want to go!" "*Mami*, my turn!" Never in their lives had they needed to go at the same time until the infamous potty chair was introduced. So I went and bought a potty seat (I would have bought an identical potty chair but ours, being a normal bathroom–and not one designed for twins–had simply no space for it).

The potty seat then became the reason for fights. Why? Because it had Elmo. There was a point when I wanted to paint that seat with black non-fading marker while Sebastián and Rodrigo were asleep. But I didn't. The novelty of the potty chair and the potty seat faded away as the days went by. If Sebastián and Rodrigo's ability to become obsessed with something and then two days later not even notice it, is any indicator of how their relationships with girls will be in the future, boy are they going to break some hearts. I hope it is a childhood thing, something they will outgrow in time.

So our next strategy was to take their clothes off before bedtime. They liked that a lot. They loved running around naked, like two Greek cupid statues come to life.

Rodrigo started going popo in the potty seat. We did not push him, he suddenly would disappear sometime after dinner and the next thing we heard was *"Mami! Papi!! Grande!!!"* He was referring to his popo, making me wonder if there is actually a male gene that dictates that size matters. Proud of himself for having produced a good-size popo, he would walk out of that bathroom with the air of a Nobel laureate stepping down from the podium after receiving the prize in the ceremony at Stockholm. His brother watched closely, but for some reason this display of honor and pride did not move Sebastián one little tiny inch closer to being motivated to accomplish something similar.

Sebastián was still pooing in his diaper. As with many other things with twins, you get to experience joy with one twin and frustration with another at the same time. I did not have to clean smeared poo on Rodrigo's butt, but I got the joy of smelling stinky poo in my fingers, even after thoroughly washing my hands, when I changed Sebastián. Time went by. Months. Rodrigo became a regular visitor to the potty, and being the neat guy he is, developed a tactic to ensure no remnants of poo would stay with him after going: he would sit, poo, then announce his achievement to the world by yelling, then get down, put his hands on the floor, butt up facing the door, so when I came in the bathroom, I saw the best angle of him and I got the privilege to clean it off. The joys of motherhood.

One day, months later, Sebastián pooed in the potty. Unexpectedly. We wondered if this was for good. Of course not. He tried it now and then, until one day I found myself thinking: I have not changed a poo diaper for Sebastián in about a week. I remembered the day when I realized I had not breast fed Sebastián in two days, he was weaning himself from me. What a different feeling that was. One was kind of nostalgic, but this one was pure happiness. And pride. Pride to see them achieve something that brought them closer to being the big boys they have wanted to become for more than a year now.

Around Christmas, Sebastián announced: I want underwear. I, the mother who cannot come to terms with the fact that I do not have babies anymore in the house, kind of ignored it. He insisted, with that quiet persistence that he uses when he knows he will get what he wants if he mentions it at the right moment, in the right place. I went out and bought underwear with trucks. He loved it. We had three days of accidents, changing five pairs of pants a day, stinky peed clothes in the washer every day. One day, in the middle of the gym class, I realized I had not put a diaper on him before leaving the house. When I reminded him, we went to the bathroom and got to do what seems to be our ritual now every time we go out: we spend half of the time in public bathrooms. They love to go at least twice at restaurant bathrooms. And boy do I feel like writing a letter to someone to ask for a simple article in their bathroom: a stool! It cannot be that hard nor costly, yet, it would benefit mother's backs and little children's experience enormously.

Sebastián then started not wetting his diaper at night at all. He now gets up in the morning and irrigates the toilet like a pump with an overload of water. Rodrigo watches him. When I ask Rodrigo: would you like to wear underwear today? He says "No thank you *Mami*." Like he is doing me a favor by saying that, meaning: no *Mami*, I really want to keep my diaper so you don't have to wash so many wet pants while I get used to underwear. Such consideration.

When I went to the bookstore a couple of months ago and saw a book called: "Potty training in a week" I laughed. I have seen little girls who stopped wearing diapers after their second birthday. My mother tells me I used *la bacinica* (old version of a potty chair) by myself when I was much younger than my kids, with that wonderful tone mothers use trying to tell you that you are not as good a mother as they were to you. I guess our policy of "laissez-faire" might not be the best in the eyes of others, but we have certainly learned that pushing these two rascals is like asking for an oak to produce pears. Hopefully Rodrigo will start wearing underwear soon. Me? I cannot believe we are now going to the store and not coming out with boxes and boxes of diapers and wipes. Life is good.

Chapter 16
Are we the Only ones?

When Sebastián and Rodrigo were little, I used to stare at mothers who yelled at their children. You see, I was a first-time mom. And even though I reject the idea of being belligerent while disciplining my kids in public, I have to say I have found myself astounded as to how draining raising twin toddlers can be. I adore them, like we all do, we all love our children to death, I admire them because they are smart and full of energy and curious and wonderfully apt to learn. I drool when they say more than five words in a row, I applaud if one of them wants to use the potty, they are so in love with their books, they nap well, and they are sweet, tender, gorgeous. BUT they are twins and they are two years old.

They are two and they run like madmen. There is no point in walking, why should they if they can get there faster if they run? They are getting creative with their toys, so now they ride the tricycle with their feet on the seat, downhill, while I have a heart attack watching them as they fly down the driveway, I leave my eyes open just enough to see how they turn, one wheel almost in the air, and make it safely to the grass, in one piece and one big smile. Of course with twins we know it only takes one of them to get one of these creative ideas, and the other twin will always follow. Always.

They are two and sometimes I feel like posting an ad hanging from our mailbox: Twins for Rent. Those are the days when they have tried my patience and wore me out. If you walk through our house you would think there was either a parade or a hurricane that had gone through it: toys everywhere, clothes strayed around, some kind of unknown sticky substance on the playroom carpet and crackers smashed on the floor in several rooms. What kills me is that they can do this in less than twenty minutes, while I am doing the dishes or on the phone trying to clear up an incorrect charge. I don't mind the mess as much as I mind the fighting. Oh, the fighting. We have taught them to share. We have taught them to take turns. They actually do both pretty well, oh, but when one of them does not feel like it, we all suffer. Their styles are quite different:

one of them just jumps on the brother and takes the toy and the other one melts on a huge tantrum when he cannot get what he wants. Is it because they are both boys? Or do all twins do the same type of pushing and shoving and crying? There must be a fantasy house for twins where there is really two of everything. If that exists, it should also have two moms (or more!).

Sometimes I wonder if we are a weird house. I wonder if we are the only ones with Christmas lights hanging from the railing of the deck because every time we dare take them down there are tears. Maybe there is another house where you cannot find a pen easily because they have all been hidden after some undiscovered artists had drawn on the walls. Is this the only house where the top tray of the dishwasher is full of sippy cups? Are we the only ones who go nuts trying to find the favorite stuffed animals, which happen to be hidden in the strangest places at the most inconvenient times, like right before nap? When Piggy or Moosey are missing, this house halts. Nobody moves. Close the doors. No one leaves the house until we find them. I think they should invent remote finders for these cases, sometimes I wished I could have pressed a button and Piggy and Moosey could beep back. Boy that would make my life much easier...

The creativity at this age has no limits. If you pair that with their eagerness to imitate you, and to please you, you can end up with a bill in your hands. Let me explain: Sebastián and Rodrigo love to play inside the mini van. We let them, we supervise them, I don't mind the hand prints in the inside of my windows as much. While I was unloading the groceries, I dared to answer the phone and start talking. How long did I talk? Three minutes? It must have been enough. The next time I am in the mini van with them, I turn on the CD player and a funny rattling noise echoes from the speakers. Definitely did not sound like Raffi (kid's music singer). We get to the grocery shop and I open the little drawer to get quarters for the cart. Empty. All my coins gone. Where? Bingo: inside the CD player! These two rascals did what I always do (put flat circle thingies in the CD player) and obeyed me (I have told them not to play with the CD's). The worst is that now they complain because we cannot listen to Raffi in the car. Oh, their short-term memory...

Some days I am tired of breaking up fights, cleaning up after them, trying to keep my cool when they go on the floor and scream, or console them when I cannot give them what they want (ice cream in the morning, for example). Other days I feel like the luckiest person in the world being part of these two little people with a strong reluctance to obey, too many ideas, and a partner to help carry them out...

"There is no point in walking, why should they if they can get there faster if they run?"

# Chapter 17
The Old Me

I want to wear my hair long again. I want to wear a size ten. I want to take a 32-mile bike ride along Millbrook or Red Hook, and feel the breeze of spring revitalize my body and my spirit. I want to go out for drinks, get a bit dizzy, go home and sleep until 11 o'clock the next day. I want to have unplanned, noisy sex. I want to take a shower with the door shut, no cold drafts sweeping in, only the sound of the falling water on my body. I would love to have a belly without the texture of a de-inflated balloon.

Things have certainly changed. My life took not only a 180-degree turn, it actually spun several rotations to become a planet in another galaxy, another reality, one that I never imagined existed, after I had Sebastián and Rodrigo. I came to be someone with responsibility for others' lives, scared to my bones that I could make a mistake that could be fatal. What if they fall from the stairs, continue to be constipated forever, don't develop normally?

Eurípides called motherhood "a powerful spell." He was right. When I became a mother I learned a type of fear that could make me shake when, at the playground I turned my head and suddenly one was missing. Where is he? Where did he go? I don't see him. Frantically looking by the trees, under the swing, by the merry-go-round, I wanted to stop time, everybody freeze, nobody moves until I find him, him, the most important thing in my life: my child. So I am not the curvy, sexy girl that used to make heads turn at happy hour. I am not the on-her-way to be manager who used to fly to wonderful faraway countries in business class.

Now I am a mother, and on top of that, a mother of twins. I have no privacy, no time to linger, no stiletto shoes. Instead I have the honor of raising two little human beings, who were given to me like two clumps of breathing clay, and it has been our task, David's and mine, to mold them into what they are becoming these days: little men. Little men who want to dress themselves, who are determined to drink from their own cup and not their brother's, who correct me when I mispronounce something in English. Little boys who are like a reflection of each other in a mirror, yet are so different between themselves: one wears underwear, the other one does not; one is a carnivore, the other one is clearly a vegetarian; one sleeps 13 hours in a row, the other one comes to our bed at 5 o'clock as if he had the Greenwich clock implanted somewhere inside of him.

So yes, I miss my younger days; now I am a very different person, but in many ways the same. If I did not have kids today, I would still be pissed at the possibility of war.

Today I am scared to the point of insomnia about the possible war not because of me, but because of Sebastián and Rodrigo. My maternal instinct tells me there has to be something we can do to avoid bombs, lethal viruses, death. I dread the day that some radiation or a strange, evil, microscopic spore could touch the innocent bodies of Sebastián and Rodrigo. I could not survive it. I want to see them grow healthy and strong. I want to see their smiles forever, in the sun, in the wind, in the water. I want to continue having the privilege of being their mother. I want to see them go to kindergarten and learn, read, absorb so many good things life has in store for them. I want to travel one day and walk the Great Wall of China with them. I want them to know that Greenpeace exists. That dolphins are intelligent. That my love for them is the reason I breathe. I don't need my old life back; I only want to keep living this one with them, and as long as they are with me, I want to make sure their world is as safe as possible. I don't want to have to pack and flee on a plane because some maniac decided to endanger our lives. I want to stay where I am with them today, in this place that has received me warmly even though I was not born here. I have fallen in love with autumns in New York, with apple orchards, and I have never seen a bird as magnificent as a blue jay. Nothing matters more to me than seeing our twins become boys, then teenagers, then adults, then parents. They gave me the chance to become a mother and thus I became one of the happiest beings on this earth, to have them in my arms, cuddled against my breast, attached to me in a link of love and survival. I hope they have children too, and then life will also be benevolent with them, they will see that having children is the most marvelous, unprecedented gift in life. And then, joined by that human chain of reproduction, we will one day sit and I will tell them of this day, when my fears of all that could not happen because of some stupid war, kept me awake in the middle of some nights.

"My life took not only a 180-degree turn, it actually spun several rotations to become a planet in another galaxy, another reality, one that I never imagined existed..."

Chapter 18

I Choose You

Yesterday I was driving, and when I stopped at a red light, I missed the little voice behind "*Mami*, you stoppin' coz is red?" I looked in the mirror and saw two empty seats. They looked so weird without Sebastián and Rodrigo's car seats, without them strapped to them, the mini van felt empty, useless. We had to switch the car seats to David's van for some reason that I don't recall (I always think part of my brain got drained through my nipples when I breast fed). The kids were home and I was without them; this normally is a reason for exhilaration, but this time, for some reason, it felt sad. The fact is, suddenly I imagined myself in this same time, but with no kids. How would my days be? What would I be doing? I would probably have continued to be a workaholic, made one more promotion, accumulated thousands more air miles. By this time of the year, I would be biking every day, all geared up like I used to, following Dave on our daily 17-mile rides. I would have an office in our house, one full room devoted to myself and no one else. We would have sex frequently, with no noise restrictions. I probably would have been to other countries for work and to vacation, made new friends, eaten delicious food, listened to other languages and continued to learned from other cultures.

What I would have missed though, cannot be compared. It was one night 3 years ago that I discovered the moon. It was a clear night with a gorgeous full moon. I was putting Rodrigo to sleep. Suddenly he looked up at the window and he stopped gurgling and remained still. In his pupils I could see the moon, a tiny little white circle that filled his whole self with wonder and awe. He was watching it for the first time, like drinking it in with his eyes. It was a magic moment, and I saw the moon with a fascination I had never felt.

I would have never grasped the difference between a kid who napped and a kid who did not. When I used to see whiny kids in stores or restaurants, I used to be annoyed and silently blamed the parents for not doing their jobs. Now I think: "That poor kid may be tired, maybe he didn't nap," and I go back to my business without giving dirty looks.

After I had twins, I developed a third arm and some of my limbs could be extended to lengths I did not know they could. That way, while holding one baby to my breast, I was able to reach the phone which was, it seemed, three feet away, in nanoseconds so that the other twin sleeping on the crib would not wake up. I also was able to use this third arm to carry the extra diaper bag, the extra bottle, the other exersaucer, and the second stroller.

I used to admire strong women at work. Decisive, brilliant, good mentors. Now my admiration has shifted to those mothers of twins who make it alone. The other night in one of our Mother of Multiples meetings, a new member asked, "Do you think I will need help when the twins are born?" Three of us jumped, "YES! Of course!" Some others in the room nodded. I told her I had my mom and my sister for the first full four months and I barely survived. But then I stayed quiet (which is not typical) and realized that other moms in the room had remained silent. I realized many of them did this alone. Now, those are my heroes. I have some good friends who had twins or triplets, and they did it alone. Some help in the beginning, but with family far away, that did not last long and they did the round-the-clock nighttime feedings alone, the endless diapering, laundry, pediatrician's appointments, pumping, caring, changing, kissing, sleeping three hours at a time for weeks, for months, they did this by themselves for most of the day, and they remain the source of my most sincere admiration. You know how they have monuments to colonels and captains and presidents in some parks. I think there should be, somewhere, one huge massive monument to the mother of twins who did it alone. Their kids are healthy and happy. Now there is a successful woman.

If I had not had twins I would have never truly appreciated the importance of being different and the respect that has to be provoked in all of us: by having one kid who is hypersensitive, and the other that basically does not feel pain; one who sleeps many hours straight and another who can barely make it to four in a row; one who lives on protein and the other pure carbohydrates; one who sees himself as a physical attachment to my body, the other who cannot wait to fly away from me. By knowing that in the end they are in essence the same: my sons, my flesh, my present, children of the world, part of the future of this Earth, I know my love is no different for either of them. I can love them both at the same time. And the chance has been given to us, as mothers of multiples, to rejoice in their differences, and love them just the same. Although sometimes

I have to admit, I want to put a sign by our house that says, "Children available for three hours; no questions asked, please take them." I have to say that yesterday a glimpse of my life without them passed before my eyes, I chose them over everything else that might have happened to me.

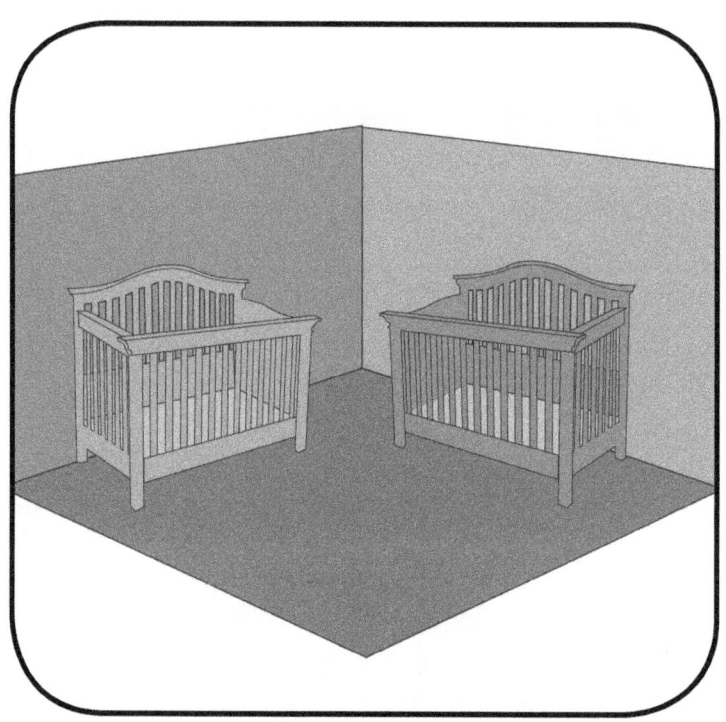

Chapter 19

Missing Them Already

Tonight Rodrigo took a shower with daddy instead of a bath. I was doing the dishes so I did not know of this, until David came afterwards to report that Rodrigo refused to take a bath. He was happy with the shower. I was surprised, then remembered his smile when we went to Cancún last year, where he spent most of the time on the beach shower, not on the waves, not on the sand, but on that bright yellow tile shower, happy to be drenched by the mini rain. So I understood a little and at the same time I was a little sad too. Will this be another bye-bye to yet another stage? In the last months they have started to be so independent that it scares me. They bring their own stool to the kitchen sink to wash their hands, they can be outside playing in the yard for a little bit of time without supervision, they decide what video they want to watch.

Early after they were born I realized that you really never know when "the last time" will be. I cannot recall the last time I sang to Sebastián before getting into bed, snuggled in my arms, looking at me with absolute adoration. I never knew when the last time they breast fed was, since they weaned themselves. I did not enjoy the last time they sat on their bouncy seats, when it started to be a bit dangerous since they were getting too big, too strong and basically bored by it. I don't miss the messy floors after every meal. Oh do I wish we had a dog in those days, to help me clean the bits and pieces, dozens of them, spread all around the floor. I miss some mornings when they would wake up early, but decided to coo in their cribs instead of calling us, that rhythmic sound of their little voices, and if you peeked in, you would see them holding on to their toes, looking at the ceiling, talking some strange tongue that only babies and fairies know.

I miss the little toddlers who would look at me in wonder when I pointed to a bird's nest. That little face with amazing surprise will never disappear from my memory. Now they are still curious and marvel at Mother Nature, but words have taken over so many aspects of our relationship. Now they use logic, funny and transparent, but sometimes they kill me with demands. Sometimes they talk incessantly. Telling them stories helps; they stop and listen. They love to hear of emperors going to other countries, of angels whispering secrets to boys in their sleep, or about baby baboons that go to Paris and climb up the Eiffel tower.

I don't miss the hassle of carrying two 2-year olds in a mini van and then the whole logistic of how to take them out one at a time avoiding the other one to scream when I disappeared into the house, and then leave the first one in the house, in a safe place, run out and get the second out of his seat, in a haste before the first one missed me and started crying. Now (if they are really interested) they even let themselves into the mini van, get in their seats, and wait for me to buckle them in. And even that, sometimes they help to do.

As I am writing this I watch my neighbors' 16-year old son drive in and I wonder if it will be a blink before Rodrigo and Sebastián get a permit and drive me around for a change. Will I be happy? Relieved? Will I miss these two little ones that right now are asleep because they swam too much in this hot summer day? As much as I complain sometimes about these tiring times, I have to say what other mothers of twins told me is true: when you have twins it is really, really hard; then it gets a bit easier, then again it gets very difficult, and then after three years of age it gets much easier. They were right. But when they were a few months old (no sleep, no rest, wide waist, yawns one minute, giggles the next) even with the invaluable help of David and my mom, sister, Clemen and friends, the days when it would get easier seemed so far away. Well, they are here. They get out of their beds by themselves in the morning, one always cheerful, the other grumpy as can be, they ask for food, they know if they are thirsty or tired, they can describe exactly the toy they are missing. No more guessing. I remember being an ace at figuring out what they wanted when they were preverbal. It seems like we moms are equipped with just the right number of guessing neurons to do that. But many times their crying and the pointing led nowhere and I felt like crying with them in despair because I was as sad as them not to know how to help them, how to interpret their sadness (they were fed, clean, changed, rested, what the heck did I miss? Why where they crying now? And while they grow, something still aches a bit. Maybe knowing we will have no more babies in this house makes me miss those little toes, that babbling before nap, the smile when they placed a block on top of the other.

I see them growing every day, inches at a time, saying full and perfect phrases using words like also, actually and if. I see pictures of a year ago and my eyes tear up, they still looked somewhat like babies, not like the little boys, mini-men, they have become. I get nostalgic perhaps because part of me has grown also. I am not the same Sofía that delivered them forty-two months ago. They have made me a better person, one that is more aware of butterflies, one that watches out for ladybugs, one that laughs hard with the clowns and likes to make rainbows when we water the flowers. I have to thank them for that, forever my kids, forever my joy.

Reborn

Chapter 20

They are here. Jack and Ben are here. Finally and with all that anticipation built around them, they came out to see the light of day for the first time on Friday. When I heard the news I was thrilled, poor Ann, forty plus weeks pregnant! *Ay ay ay.* But now she and her husband gave us all one of the most wonderful bits of news in the world: the babies are here! Suddenly I wanted to be there, right there with them, see the cuties, hug them, carry them, help my friend in whatever way I could. But then the romantic view of new parents amongst clouds disappeared and I remembered what it was really like after delivering twins: you are drugged, he is still in shock, the babies sleep most of the time, you and your husband need some time to recover. Maybe a year or two actually. But the truth is that as you recover from the whole ordeal of the birth, the next wave comes over you: look at them! How cute, how adorable, ouch, that latching really hurts. Is there anything anybody can do to take this three inch-wide opening I have in my belly and bring it back to me when it is healed? Can anyone tell me what this belly I still have is? Didn't someone tell my belly the babies are out? How can I reinstall my body? I would love to have it back to where it was before I got pregnant, how about in two hours? Anyone? Help! I remembered being on the hospital bed, balloons floating, and visitors in and out, the phone rang, yet I was in a far away zone. I smiled and answered, but the painkillers were truly working and my brain was gone. Three years later, I have actually just started to recover.

In the hospital, I started a huge transformation: from a walking womb to a walking breast. Let the feedings begin. The pump, the late hours, the babies who were kind of insatiable at times. The little toes, the wide open eyes, "hi *Mami*, so this is how you look from the outside, *hola*." As I held Ben today I had that sensation that overwhelms you when you are a mom: you need to protect. There is this instinct well below your skin level, that yells from each pore "Here I am, don't worry, nothing will happen to you while I am around." And so we feed, we change, we sing lullabies, we try five dozen different bottle nipples, we spend money like we had tons of it, we cry when they cry, we are reborn the day they came out of us. Because babies are the exact definition of hope: there it is, cozily wrapped in cute blankies, a bundle of aspirations. Ben and Jack can be anything, and it is up to us to bring them up all the time: up to the breast, up to their tummies, up to their butts when they sit, up to their feet, and then fly, fly away my son, the world is vast and holds so much for you, go get it! Let me polish those wings, go, let me see you and come back and then to tell me how your adventures are going. I will always be there. Because I am your mom, he is your dad, we will always be here for you.

I had the privilege to help with one feeding while we were visiting in the hospital today. The women in the room sent the boys and men out to do something manly: pass a baby carriage from our car to the other. The three women in the room, Mom Chara, Ann, and I got to our task. Mom Chara held Jack, I took Ben, we checked diapers, changed one, fed one with a bottle and the other one had Ann for some afternoon snack. Suddenly I realized the three of us were all mothers of twins, a silent bond knitted us together, the three of us in love with the babies, the three of us naturally skilled, like all mothers in the world, to take care of our babies.

Ann also reminded me how the first tool we have as moms is our instinct. While I thought Ben was not hungry and just sleepy, she kept working at it, and when we gave up and I put him back to his bassinet, oh my, the crying, good lungs! I brought him back to mama and sure enough, two seconds later he was attached like only a newborn can attach to his mom. And so she enters the hall of Mothers of Twins, with her brand new instinct. In these first months, that instinct will guide her like a bright light would guide the blind on a tricky road. She will know what Ben and Jack need although others hesitate or even give contradictory advice. She will hear how the babies turn or gurgle, even if there are three walls between them. She will live fascinated by their beauty, resilience, the wonderful miracle they are, and we will all sit by her side, illuminated by the glow of her happiness. Because we know they have been through a lot, years of yearning, and then, suddenly, viola! THEY ARE HERE!

While I held Ben today I murmured quietly: "Welcome little one, you have no idea how much we have all been waiting for you and your brother. We are so lucky to have you with us. It is an honor, and we intend to live up to it."

"Suddenly I realized the three of us were all mothers of twins"

Chapter 21
Saturday in Darien

We just came back from visiting our friends Ann and Dave. Every time we go it is the same story: we plan to stay shorter and we end up staying longer. Something about the house, about their hospitality, about how comfortable we are around them. Coming back, we just took Sebastián and Rodrigo out of the car, put their pajamas on while they were still half asleep from the trip up, and left them on their beds completely exhausted. No need to tiptoe out of their room; they were gone by the time we finished changing them. David mentioned that they had been good boys today. How couldn't they? They were in heaven: peanut butter Reese's cups, dogs galore, babies, potato chips, the park, a visit to the ice cream shop and two videos. Life was good to them today.

I was also in heaven. I got to hold Ben and Jack again, already ten weeks old! Jack is chubby as can be, a solid ball of goodness, strong, double chin, very content if he was fed and left to rest. Ben has long arms and legs, sparkling blue eyes surrounded by a curly wave of long lashes that make him look like one of those baby faces you see on parents' magazine covers. When I had him in my arms, he liked full attention: he did not like it when I talked to someone else or when I changed the position where he was comfortable or if I decided he was done with the bottle since he had not sucked on it for a while. And who am I to say what he wants? Babies know what they want; we adults are here on Earth to guess. Is he tired? Is he hungry? Is he bored? Is he wet? Did he go poopoo? When did he eat last? Which one is his bottle? Is this Ben's milk? Or Jack's milk? Where was that burping cloth? Is he feverish? Where did I leave the binky? Should I put him in his bouncy chair or in his crib? Maybe he is hot. Maybe he is cold. Are these socks too thick? How can I help him?

And so we go tumbling those first months, like a foreigner in a land where no one seems to have a dictionary to understand these babies' language. The baby industry has come up with wonderful artifacts. The monitors are now a must have. Vibrating chairs are a blessing. Bottles that, thanks to five attachments, do not let air go into the babies' tummies, are complicated but effective. Musical mobiles that help them go to sleep even though we feel that if we listen to the same Brahms lullaby one more time we could go mad. One thing someone has to come up with is a crystal ball to read babies minds.

We decided to bring our dog, Tula, because I, as a mother who wants her sprouts to be social early in life, thought it would be good for her to meet their dog, Ruby. And so I sat with her in the back seat on the way down, because being only nine weeks she gets a bit nervous riding in the car. When we got there and I saw Ruby, Tula looked smaller than ever to me. It must be that Ruby weighs probably 80 pounds more than our little puppy. Tula was not afraid nor impressed though, she immediately tried to play with her. The dwarf and the mammoth. Ruby was like a gentle giant, looking at her with some compassion, and some curiosity, like; "Do you grasp the concept that if I play like that with you I might actually hurt you without even wanting to?" But Tula kept following her in the park, trying to make her run and dying to wrestle with her. Luckily Ruby was a thoughtful lady who passed on the offer.

In the park, Sebastián and Rodrigo took Lynn, David and I, oh and Tula, to a ride on a truck to Timbuktu. David had to fix two tires before we left on our trip, and we had to stop to shop for a carrot cake on the way there. After the excursion was over, Rodrigo went climbing on a play dome and almost reached the top, a good 8 feet off the ground. When they do things like that, and I fear for their lives, I realize that almost four years after they were born the guessing game is not over for us yet, and probably never will. What if he falls? He can break something if he did. What if I go and bring him down? No, I better leave him and let him do it by himself. But what if he hurts himself? Look at him, he is swinging, oh please, don't let him fall. Nope, he is back in control again, now he wants to climb higher. "Rodrigo, please be careful," is all I can mutter when what I really mean is "Rodrigo, please get down and stop making my knees tremble." But he loves heights, and he is pretty good with them, while his brother is much more cautious.

Another thing where their roles invert is that Sebastián is typically fearless and Rodrigo is very wary. I look at Ben and Jack in their double stroller and wonder who is going to be fearless, who is not; who is going to be hypersensitive, who is going to have a high threshold for pain; who will nap like a prince, who will want to be up all the time? Maybe it is not that they are born like that, but that as twins they mold each other into different persons because they coexist all the time.

Sometimes I feel like Rodrigo tends to be more this or that only because Sebastián is not. Like a way to stamp his personality, like a way to demonstrate his individuality. Are we all like that in the end? Do we grow up seeing others and then making up our own mind as to what we like and what we don't, and then act in consequence? I remember being a good student, but was I an 'A student' because I liked it or because none of my brothers and sisters were? What happens with singletons? Do they get to grow up exactly the way they were meant to be? Freud, where are you?

Lynn was there, our dear friend who is always such a pleasure to see and talk with. She is one of those friends who will give an honest opinion without hesitating for a half-second and she has the ability to do it harmlessly. Plus, talking with her is always an intelligent proposition, because her brain works quick and concisely. On the other side, there is this sweet side of her that makes me feel sad because she lives in DC and we get to see her not as often as we would love. But she comes often to everyone's joy. When I asked why she came to NY she said it was for a seminar. Not to attend, but to speak. She mentioned our friend Tim got a new permanent job, managing people with more responsibility. Ann showed us a prestigious magazine that featured her work as an architect in the gorgeous renovation of an apartment in Park Avenue. We all keep moving. We are past the times when we went to sit in a seminar or when we are told what to do. Now we get to speak as experts and to tell others what to do. Dave said we are not getting old: we *are* old.

But then again, we had our own party, and as we sat for dinner we raised our glasses to numerous occasions: Lynn's birthday, my birthday, Dave and Ann's anniversary. Ann made us laugh when she said that this year her resolution was to be auto sufficient. She had an epiphany in the hospital when she was in the bathroom and there was a nurse with her. Where is my privacy? Why can I not do anything alone anymore? This was the moment of truth in the whole ordeal of incapacitated state that you go through when you have two growing babies under your belly. You cannot get out of the car alone. You cannot climb stairs unless someone pushes you from behind. You get asked while doing the groceries; "So when are you due? Two weeks?" No, three more months you reply with a grin. Getting out of bed is an equivalent of pushing a hippo from a deep water hole. Your toes? Where are they? Haven't seen them in months.

I was amazed when at one point this afternoon Ann disappeared for a little bit and suddenly reappeared on the stage with mascara on, lips shinning and her beautiful hair down. I do get time to brush my hair once a week, she stated. I remember days when I did not have time to shower. Days when these two were fussy as can be and I wanted to cry with them, just sit there and surrender. Days when I knew no one fully understood me and my concerns for my children, the most important beings on this earth. How can the nurse make me wait so long on the phone? What is the neighbor thinking when he is mowing his lawn exactly at their nap time?

I guess being a parent for the first time kind of erases all sense of sanity. Not to mention when you are caring for two little babies at the same time. So there was Ann radiant. She lost all her weight within two weeks of giving birth. To this day, I cannot say that, and it has been almost four years. Self-indulgence runs in my family and even at almost forty, I cannot say I have found a way to defeat that "gene". Not that I have tried really hard either. Ann wanted to have a picture of Dave and her with the babies. "Later" she said. "Now" I recommended, seeing the babies were content and the moment was right. You have to take advantage of such moments in twin world, before one of them falls asleep, or cries, or simply does not feel photogenic at that particular moment and decides to scream for the camera and have his tonsils displayed for posterity. So we took, ah, let's say 20 pictures, of which I am sure one of them is going to be gorgeous and years from now we will see it and remember this sunny September afternoon, when two sets of twin boys, two lady dogs, and five friends came together to enjoy life together.

"Babies know what they want; we adults are here on Earth to guess. Is he tired? Is he hungry? Is he bored? Is he wet? When did he eat last? Which one is his bottle?"

Chapter 22

Wild Flowers

Today was special. It came with one of the nicest moments in my life: my twin boys gave me flowers. They were not roses, they were not fancy, no cellophane or card–they were wild flowers. Which was very suiting for the carriers, because at three and a half, they can be quite uncivilized at times.

I recently read a definition of a toddler: a small being of extreme stubbornness and complete lack of sense. There is a definition. Although Sebastián and Rodrigo are over that difficult age, it seems like yesterday when we were still dealing with major tantrums and unthinkable, not to mention creative, mischief. Now they are less adamant about making me feel stupid (how could I not understand how important it is that one gets to drink from the blue cup and the other from the yellow cup), insensitive (but *Mami*, I really really really need to watch a video) and cruel (just one more book *Mami*, one more). Now that they are talking, they talk all day; they say phrases that start with "if" and "perhaps." They tell me full made-up stories of boats and crocodiles, fairies and magic carpets. The stories go on and on, or shall I say on and off, because while Sebastián normally starts them, Rodrigo takes over while Sebastián thinks of other elements missing, and then continues to let Rodrigo do the grand finale of the tale. We sit in mute, watching them like a tennis match, until we simply lost track of who was the main character: the big bad wolf, the caterpillar or the whale? These little ones who now want to understand where squirrels sleep and love to move to see their shadow follow, brought me flowers today.

And I am so happy I had kids. Not that I don't feel that happiness constantly, since we all know how maternity can make you experience joy in levels you never knew, along with frustration of course. You learn you can love to an extent you did not even imagine before, and you also learn that your patience is not exactly endless. I decided earlier this year to stop going to the office and work from home, which has turned to have as many cons as pros. One of the cons is that if I have long calls to be on, it is really hard for Sebastián and Rodrigo to stay occupied away from me. I am pretty sure when we give birth there is a metal plank that stays with us, and a strong magnet stays with them; these two are only attracted to each other in a one-to-one link, or shall I say two-to-one link? So even though they are in a complete separate part of the house with Clementina, they eventually come in my office and demand attention, and what little boy wouldn't? In these cases, Clemen (my definition of a super hero) runs interference and plays with them or takes them for a walk like today. I saw them depart the house with her and ran inside to be on this call, which was complicated and kind of difficult, basically because the people that I work with --who are all full-timers (and not a part timer like I am), often ladies with no kids, or quite ambitious gentlemen, all devoted viciously to their jobs-- work at a pace that I can barely keep up with. All they do is sit in front of a computer in a confined office for ten hours a day. They don't have to deal with house chores, grocery shopping, music class, library visits or playtime with two quite active little dwarfs in those same ten hours. So I basically feel like a midget running a marathon with seven feet-tall professional athletes. That is my work life these days.

Just before I was done with the call, I see them coming back from their walk, smiling and running up the driveway. The call was over, I quickly hang up and go to greet them at the door, and suddenly I see them walking to me with two bunches of yellow and white wildflowers. "We bot' you fawers *Mami*." I kneeled and stayed there savoring those few seconds, when you are shocked and you realize this is a good shock, this surprise is good, you are delighted, and as they saw me transform from their regular mom into an extremely delighted one, they smiled and came to hug me, and I had petals on my hair, saliva on my cheek and two of the greatest gifts of life in between my arms. How can such a little act be so powerful? Clementina then added "they cut them themselves; I did not tell them to do it." Sebastián and Rodrigo were also a little shocked too at my reaction; and then they were elated they had made me so happy. When daddy came home later, the first thing they told him was "*Mami* likes fawers daddy." And here they are, on a clear vase, on my desk.

I wonder what else is in stock for me with these two; I am afraid they might not turn out to be exactly what I expect them to be; I see teenagers and my skin crawls just thinking one day I might be the least liked person in their lives. They will avoid me and try to be only with their friends. I will be the one they need to leave to fly into the world. I will no longer be the person they want to bring flowers to. But for now, let me be happy. Let me look at this bunch of colors on my desk and be the happiest mom in the world. Let me enjoy these two princes who are often saving me from dragons when I am their princess, who ask me to come set up the paint and paper for them, who protest if we have to stop reading books because it is time for a shower. Today they need me and I am lucky enough to be here for them. Even after these flowers wither.

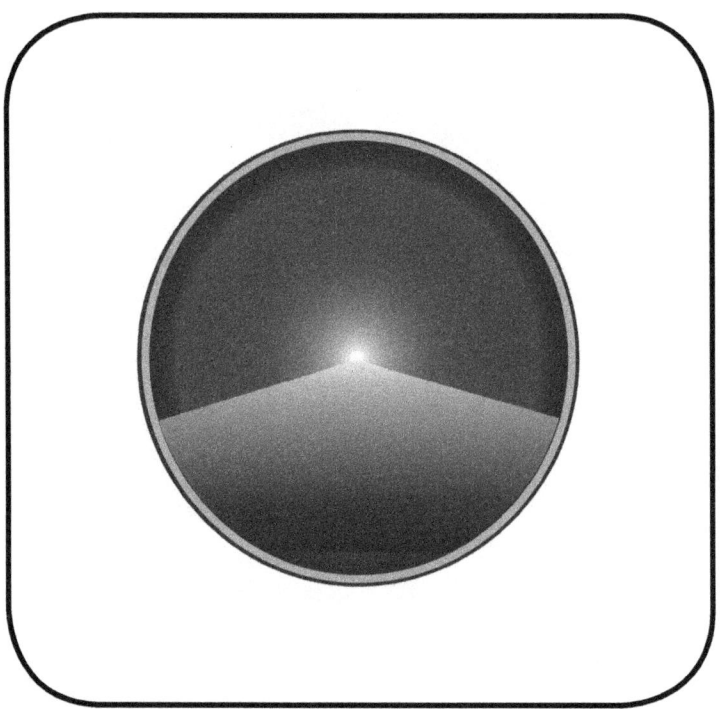

Chapter 23: There is Hope

The other day we were at a diner when we saw a couple come in with two young twin boys and two older kids. While they sat down, going through the not-so-easy process of shedding coats and settling down with the bunch, I thought to myself with excitement; "Oh my, twin boys! Like ours!" The only big fat difference was the age of course. The newcomers were at least half the age than ours, and that, we all moms of multiples know, is a huge difference. So as I was taking Sebastián and Rodrigo to the bathroom to wash their hands, the mother of the other twins noticed us and asked the never-ending question from strangers: Are they twins? And we chatted for a little bit, and I saw the distress in her eyes and the desperation on his when they wanted to know: Does it get easier? I sighed and for the first time since I had my twins I said: Yes, it does get easier. Hers were one and a half years old; mine are going to be four in two months, so yes, definitely, positively, undoubtedly it gets easier. I thought of all the moms who, like this woman and like myself not long ago, felt like a drowning swimmer who barely had time to catch some air afloat and then was dragged underwater again by spills, tantrums, fevers, lack of sleep or pure exhaustion. I had to get to the bathroom since our food was coming, so I could not tell all of this to the mom:

One day your house will be bottle-free. There will be no more milk everywhere and all the time. I remember when my twins were babies there was milk everywhere: on their clothes, on the couch, on my bra, in the fridge, in the sink, in the cribs, this house was a branch of the Milky Way. Two breasts, two bottles, two babies who were hungry now and soon afterwards, demanded me to bring out my nipples to the point that I remember one day thinking: I am not sure why I care to wear a shirt. So the milk was suctioned, poured, served, warmed, vomited. It was a source of benefic soothing or of ultimate frustration when it wouldn't come out fast enough. But there will be a day when, you will see, milk will actually only come out of the fridge, from a gallon container, at scheduled meals like breakfast, lunch and dinner.

You will go one day to the supermarket and come out with groceries, but no diapers. I will never forget my first time: coming out of the supermarket, I could not believe that there was not one single massive box of diapers in the cart. We were done with them! Even with the ones for overnight. Where were the days of twenty diaper changes a day? Changing a diaper eventually becomes a skill that you master to a point that you can do it while talking on the phone or holding the other baby. You do it virtually in your sleep, and when you wake up you find yourself thinking: did I change him or not? You go to the crib, and voila, the diaper is not that full, so you definitely changed it during the night although you have no full recollection of it. You learn the Greco-Roman way of pinning down the enemy when the babies hit six months and the least that is on their minds is to stay still while you change them. Diapers can account for at least a third of your weekly garbage can. The smell in the house sometimes makes you wonder if someone will come up with an air freshener to eliminate bad baby smells. And then they grow, you all go through the endless amounts of detergent and patience it takes to potty train two at a time, and one day you, your house, your car, your trips, they are all diaper-free. Hooray!

One day they will actually stop fighting twice an hour. The hair pulling, the pushing, the biting, all of it will go away. They will learn their actions have consequences and will learn to wait their turn. You will also see them apologize to each other, and mean it. Those days of you on the floor soothing two hurt babies, who are both wailing of physical pain and emotional distress because 'how come his own twin hit him?', those days will end. They will still fight, mind you, but they will do so as a last resort, after trying to come to a common agreement and after all ways of convincing have been exhausted.

There will come a day when you will actually be able to socialize with other adults at parties. For their first three years, every gathering we used to attend would typically end up David in charge of one kid, I in charge of the other, following them around, making sure they did not fall downstairs, spill juice on their new outfits or drink from someone's beer left unattended. We used to end up exhausted and leaving without being able to finish any short conversation we started with anyone.

One day you will be able to go to the bathroom alone, even shower alone, without the two guests sitting first row watching you, asking you questions, or simply sitting there amazed by the fact that you don't have a penis.

One day they will be able to go outside by themselves. They will yell; "*Mami*! We are going to ride our bikes!" They will fly in front of your eyes, get their zip-up shoes on, put their jackets, find their hats, reach the knob and open it to go out there, and they will not run to cross the street or wander where they should not. You will be finishing the dishes and watching them out there, both entertaining each other, a long-lived tradition in twins, inventing races or fighting dragons in make-believe castles.

The guessing game will come to a halt when they start talking. Little by little they will be able to tell you exactly what they want, and you will stop trying to speculate "what the heck does this kid want?" Is he hungry? Tired? Thirsty? Does he want me to put him down for a nap? Leave him alone? Is his diaper wet? Why is he still crying? With the arrival of language, your life will get much, MUCH easier, and you will enter the realm of invented words, make-up stories, and wonderful tales of how their day went that they entertain their father when he comes home after work. You will hear their account of events and realize that hey, it was not such a bad day after all!

If you have been blessed with a child who sleeps in short periods at a time, rest reassured he or she will one day elongate those periods so that you will be able to sleep at least seven hours in a row. For years, we slept four hours at a time, all of us, except for Sebastián who admirably so, found a way to sleep through his brother waking up often and to this day, for a reason that continues to be unknown to us. Mysteries unsolved, like some others in every house of twins.

One day you will see them drinking from open cups, and you will finally have no toys in every single room. Most of their toys will be in the bedrooms or in the playroom!

Other things will also end that you will miss. You will miss being able to dress them up to your wish. The outrageous combinations Sebastián and Rodrigo choose at times makes me wonder if I would be better off just having jeans and white t-shirts available in their drawers. You will miss their cooing, their sweet voice at dawn while they are sucking at their big toe and looking up at the stars painted in the ceiling of their room. They will not stay quiet and let you go while daddy is holding them when you go to your monthly Mothers of Twins meeting, instead at least one of them will scream and make a drama fit for the New York City Opera. You will miss their naps, those two glorious hours in the middle of the day when you had time to rest, catch up or do e-mail, and they were not a reason to worry because they were fast asleep. You will see babies who are crawling and remember how cute your own used to be when they were that age, how much you miss the eternal struggle to get up, hold on to furniture and eventually walk. Now their aims are more mental. There are ABC's to learn, stories to follow from start to end, games that involve counting and the eternal waiting to be able to ride on a school bus. Because in a way, all they are doing is growing, and we are here to help them through the jungle that can be shedding skins as they get bigger, becoming these awesome kids that marvel us all with their ingenuity, their intelligence, their dedication to learn more. We are here to be their companions and guides. And although the journey at times can be long and dark, believe me, there is light at the end of the tunnel. And it is a bright and gorgeous day when you get there.

"Does it get easier? I sighed and for the first time since I had my twins I said: Yes, it does get easier."

Sad Iron

Chapter 24

I just saw Iron-Jawed Angels and as the movie was finishing, this incredible pain came all over me. It was not my lower back, which tends to act up early in the morning and late at night. It was not my stomach complaining for how much food I have put into it this weekend. It was not my neck because I have been lying crooked to allow Tula a little more space for her legs that imminently will be longer than mine, the growing puppy she is. It was a pain that has been silent, but always present since my third sonogram when I was pregnant: I will never have a girl to raise.

That day, I learned I was having two boys, not a girl and a boy like my dream had told me. So I will never sit on a Sunday night, with a young woman in the chair to my right, watching this wonderful movie, talking about how women can change the world, how uteri are not in contradiction with brains, how the fight in this country is on Chapter XXX and in other countries it is just in the Preface; it has just started to be written. I will never be able to instill that sense of pride and justice into a little girl. I have twin boys, they are four, I am forty this year, I refuse to become pregnant again and be sick for six months, vomiting, dehydrated and wishing every day was over sooner. I am not so brave, or so crazy. We could adopt, we have discussed that, but other interests always come first: we are not financially as sound as we thought, adoption is not cheap, plus David and I have not yet agreed on the age; he wants a one year old, I want the baby from birth. But just thinking of getting my tired self out of bed again twice every night to soothe a teething baby is the equal in my mind to the idea of walking on my knees for kilometers to see la *Vírgen de Guadalupe* in Mexico City. I can't, I won't. I am clearly a coward.

So the price for being a coward is the sad moment I just had on the sofa, alone, as this astonishing story of feminine courage and stubbornness unfolded before my widened eyes. "The film shows how these activists broke from the mainstream women's-rights movement and created a more radical wing, daring to push the boundaries of political protest to secure women's voting rights in 1920" is how the website describes the movie; to me it was also a movie about female spirit that will not be subdued. These girls were so smart, so devoted, so relentless, that while the movie is ending you feel like you have to get up and do something meaningful with your life. None of the women who were the leaders of this movement had children, according to the movie. None were distracted by relationships with men. I do think they missed out on the great experience of being a mother, but they were completely devoted to their cause, and I just wished I had a little girl to share with the inspiration that perspired from the television tonight. But that just does not seem possible, not now, not in the future. Unless of course, there is a turn of fate and I am named the guardian of a girl from *La Tenería,* the ranch where my grandmother was raised, in Central Mexico, where dozens of children go to school and have to share a crayon, after a walk between three and four miles, in an unpaved road that Sebastián and Rodrigo described as a "construction site" when we visited recently. This is a place where there are no phone lines, but they are really not needed, because everybody knows everybody, they are all one huge family, and even in poverty, these people are happier than many other people I know who have cars and go to amusement parks every year. They know what to lack something is; something as basic as food or running water. So when they do have food and running water, their day is better than others. They smile and they sit with you at their table and share their meal with you. It is also a place where women are often battered, where there is disappointment when a woman does not have a male baby, where women still look down if the man of the house is talking. That is where the work of equality is needed. Where the Preface of a story like Iron-Jawed Angels could at least be started. They are eons away from how things are in this country, although I read that in one of the recent elections in the US there were 16 million unregistered women and 21.7 million women who were eligible to vote in the US who did not. I do not know statistics from Mexico, but I am sure they are proportionally either the same or worse.

And all this, I will never be able to talk about with a girl, blood of my blood, with my genes in her, in my capacity to influence her view, to make sure she realizes that there are so many advantages to being a woman, capable of caring and strength, of loyalty and pure fun. As women we can joke and be serious at the same time, we can make a man come to his knees while making him feel like the most important being on the planet; we can breastfeed and read an interesting article in the New York Times at the same time (not that I ever did, but I know women who do).

So tonight in my rollercoaster of emotions, my soul clenched by a powerful story, I almost cried because it reminded me of all the other things I will never be able to do. I will never teach my non-existent daughter to cook *sopa de tortilla, or chilaquiles con pollo.* I will never sit and talk about menstrual periods and their ancient relationship to the moon cycles. I will never make up a story together with her as to how God, as a Woman, would have created the world. I will never see her fluttered with excitement on her first date. I will never braid her thick dark hair. My shopping for kids clothes will continue to be this fast pass at the girls department, full of fun colors, bright designs and flowers, to then face the serious dark greens, inevitable navy blue and pale browns, with truck designs of the boys apparel. No one will ever learn to take care of an infant the way I do, to worry as a mother like I do. Like my grandmother did, like my own mom did. Because with me, the only daughter of my mother, finishes a lineage of women who have not been famous for being particularly quiet or tamable.

Someone might say: your sons will learn all that from you. Yes, undoubtedly. With any luck, they will learn from me the strong belief that men are important to letting women feel and be free. Not men like your brother or my uncle, men as in the systems they create, as male corporations, male politics, and male professions. If I am successful, my sons will one day learn, and actually enjoy, listening to women, opening their souls to what they have to say and let the message go right in to the deep pool of their beliefs. They will let themselves get infested by some of the typical female anarchism and joy in speaking their minds. And if that happens, maybe I have served a good cause.

Chapter 25 Beds

The Relaxed Bed: I worked all day, fully dedicated to my job. The gym was an every morning 7-8 AM ritual. I slept late, went out, had drinks, but most of all, I used to sleep in on weekends.

The Let's-get-pregnant Bed: different positions would enhance the possibility of getting us pregnant. We did them all. I guess they worked pretty well, because one morning, the test showed two red lines: we were going to have a baby!

The Twinshock Bed: I was bleeding that morning. We were rushed to the hospital, images of going through the horror of losing an unborn baby were daunting us like ghosts on a scary movie. Then the sonogram showed that the bleeding was contained, and "Oh! See that? Maybe you should know there are two healthy heartbeats here." That night we went from awe to fear to over joy to excitement to tears to pure terror. We were in shock. Sometimes we still are.

The Overloaded Bed: I weighed 220 pounds the day I gave birth. Compress that by noting that my height is 5'0. Five, Zero. My belly was an exploding planet with things moving inside like the crust of the Earth which is alive. Two baby boys inside me were growing, kicking, expanding, and complaining for the lack of space. So was I! My poor husband had to move out of the bed early in the pregnancy, at least one of us got to rest at night. With the five nightly visits to the bathroom and the endless task of getting comfortable (a word that is a joke after the sixth month of all twin pregnancies), I was not letting him rest. My bed was lacking a key piece of structure: a beam on the ceiling supporting an automated hook that would hinge to my pajama pants and help me get up. If only someone created one.

The Sleep Deprived Bed: Sebastián and Rodrigo arrived after 35 weeks of my body being a wreck. I had so many stitches it was not funny. I tried to get comfortable in bed, but I don't know what it was that made that task impossible. The c-section wound, parts of my body in unbearable pain, the hyper swollen lactating glands that actually hurt, the blankets wet with milk or the back pain. However, all these ailments seem to vanish when facing my need to sleep, so I normally hit the pillow and went right to sleep. And then, it seemed like ten minutes later, a baby cry. In the distance, quiet, persistent, making me come back from my drowsy rest, I needed to get up and breastfeed one of the babies. Then the other, then change one, then change the other, then put him down in the crib, then try to rest some more, then open a present that arrived in the mail, then talk on the phone with someone who wants to help (got a milking breast? Come over!), then do laundry, then a baby cries again, feed, change, wash, sleep, cry, oh, this is hard.

The Exhausted Bed – After a number of months you have it all figured out. You know what to do depending on how they cry, you know what baby needs more soothing than the other, you know the hints they give you when they need to nap, you know how to mix formula, pump like a pro, and change diapers in two minutes flat. You are able to sleep more than four hours in a row; life is starting to be good. And suddenly, out of nowhere, these two adorable creatures start growing teeth. That means you often have to get up the same number of times as in the beginning because gums hurt, we don't remember that, apparently for some insane reason Nature never thought of making teeth growth a day time activity, no sir, it apparently happens mostly at night. So now your sleep deficit, which had accumulated quite significantly in the last few months and was starting to be not in the red numbers anymore, is deepening again, and you think, "Will I endure this? How many hours of sleep do I actually need to function without driving through a red light or yelling at the slow cashier who apparently does not acknowledge that my baby is crying and I need to get back home to feed him." Your marriage is on the edge with all these new tasks to take care of two babies. At the same time, not to mention the enormous responsibility you suddenly feel, especially if you are a first-time mom. Sex? What is that?

Other beds then come. The gurgling bed, the haunted bed (*Mami*, I am afraid of the dark), the Himalaya bed (all piled up on top of me of dad), the bouncing bed, but forever then on, it is hopefully a good bed...

"Oh! See that? Maybe you should know there are two healthy heartbeats here."

Chapter 26: Lies

I just came back from meeting Jackie. She is a forty-something woman pregnant with twins, best friend to my good friend Lynn. Lynn had Ann, another mother of twins and me, meet her for dinner to talk about what else? Twins! Having twins, carrying twins, feeding twins. I caught myself getting dressed for this dinner trying to look pretty. Especially after having my twins, try to look presentable. Looking sexy, attractive, seductive has long been a thing of the past. So I was really surprised to see myself putting a real effort into looking pretty, until I thought, "Maybe I just want her to see that, even after having twins, one can still be beautiful."

I know many mothers of all kinds (singletons, twins, triplets) that did not loose their lovely figures and did not add any wrinkles to their face after giving birth. Not my case. I look at pictures of me barely six years ago and this good-looking, curvy, sexy girl looks at me from my picture, surrounded by handsome friends in Paris cheering with full glasses of wine, like saying: this was you, what the heck happened to me? She looks at me, and my flabby tummy, my dyed hair, my not-so-firm-anymore figure, and is estranged, because her, the Sofia five years ago and the Sofia of today are very different persons.

The one back then was in love with her career, darn good at it, making it to the top with no problem, partying on Fridays in Buenos Aires after a hard week of work, going to transpersonal psychology conferences in Warsaw and wearing a two piece bathing suit at the beach. I am now a mother of twins. I am a part-time, work at home, housewife, who raises with her husband two gorgeous four-year olds, and our lives revolve around that: being parents. Call me whatever you want, but first I am a mom, then I am whatever else you wish. Sebastián and Rodrigo take precedence in all my decisions, and I live day to day with them, teaching them how not to make noise when they chew, praising them when they help make breakfast, asking them to please stay in their beds all through the night. I am obsessive and probably neurotic, and all these things that I do for them are in great part to them, but in great part also for me.

Being a mother is one of the big last things I will do in my life, as tragic as that sounds. I might write a book, adopt a Mexican girl, create a non-profit organization to help teach poor kids in Mexico how to write and read, but none of these future and possible experiences will ever compare to having my two boys. So tonight, as I left the restaurant, I feel I gave Jackie a disservice. We talked about gynecologists, bouncy seats, room arrangements, breastfeeding. She asked about the delivery, we told them our stories, both c-sections, none of them pleasant experiences. We told her about the emotional roller coaster of having two at a time, but truly, did I tell her everything I wished somebody had told me before? I did not tell her about the drastic change your life takes in all aspects, excluding nothing, the moment you learn you are pregnant, let alone when the radiologist tells you: your bleeding is under control, however, you two should know that there are two healthy beating hearts in here. WHAT? You go into twinshock and I personally think I am still under that mode. What do you mean twins? You are baffled, overjoyed until you realize this is something you were not prepared for, how are you going to do this? Are you even ready to be a mom? Will you be capable of rearing two children a the same time?

I did not tell her the truth about my fears. I remember being absolutely terrified about delivery. I had nightmares: I would wake up drenched in sweat after these horrible images filled my nights. I did not tell her about the stretch marks she will have, the extra skin that will always hang from her belly no matter how many sit-ups she does. I did not tell her how much my nipples hurt the first week, how the stitches on my belly were unbearable, how for five days after the c-section I had the worse stomach pains in my life. I did not tell her I could not get out of the hospital bed after the two days I was there, and how I cried when the doctor came to discharge me, what do you mean I need to go? I can't! Don't you see me? Everything hurts, I cannot walk, I have not got a grip on the latching thing, and you need to keep me here until we all agree I am in good condition to go home. He was horrible (mind the hormonal state in those days please) and sent me home despite my strong opinions. The night before my milk had come down and I woke up in this puddle of warm liquid that the nurse had to explain to me. And from that moment on, I was a liquid producer: there was liquid coming out from everywhere, including tears rolling down my eyes. My back hurt like nothing before, the size of my breasts had doubled in forty-eight hours, I was unable to sleep and I had not even made it home to be with my kids alone. Nobody understood me, but my mom pampered me: I share her over-sensitiveness and we understand each other. So we went home, and I know if David had not been so involved since the beginning, and if my mom had not been there to help us, I would have gone nuts. And I know moms that do this literally by themselves.

My friend Mike had triplets the day before I had my twins. He and his wife Kathy had help for a couple of weeks, then she was on her own, and she handled marvelously and kept her sanity too. I am a wimp. I am nobody to be compared to because to this day I do not know anyone who can complain so much and feel so much pain. So abnormal as I was, the whole experience brought to me the highest joy that I have ever experienced. Being a mom is a drug that I am still high on. Don't ask me things like: what toys did you boys like the most when they were one, because I will not stop talking. When I have to go to meetings at work, inevitably in the middle everything I will be thinking of what are Sebastián and Rodrigo doing right now: if the meeting is longer than two hours I need to get out and call home. I am neurotic, and I see mothers of fifteen month-olds who drop them off at daycare in the morning, pick them up in the afternoon, put them to bed, and next day do it again. I actually envy them a bit. I am absolutely sure their kids will grow up to be healthy, intelligent human beings, just like mine. Although mine will have a higher chance to have to go into therapy because of an overbearing mom. I promise I will chip in for the cost of that.

So tonight as I sat across from Jackie, seeing her twenty-week pregnant belly, there was a moment when I thought, "I cannot tell her anything, she has no idea, I don't have words to prepare her." Words fail to express those 30 seconds you are sitting in the babies' room, after they had fallen asleep, and the early dawn light starts to drape the sky outside of bright orange, reaching the forms of those two bundles, deep asleep, completely trusting they are going to be fine because you are there. And you cry, you cry tears of absolute joy, because life could not have been better to you by giving you the privilege of having not one, but two kids at the same time. You cry because you feel completely unready for the responsibility. Up until then you were competent of taking care of yourself, but taking care of someone else, especially if you had not have a simple dog or golden fish to look after in twenty years, seems like a monstrous task for which you have no skills. But your body pulls through the exhaustion, your friends come over and warm up your cold tea while you feed the babies like my friend Janet did, your mom feeds you spoonfuls of vegetable soup while one of the babies is attached to your right breast. You and your husband make it through.

Months go by and you look back and wonder how you did it, but you did it. You do what all the mothers have done for millennia: you create and protect life. Apart from passing on your genes and fulfilling a personal dream, you become part of the great drama of life on this Earth, putting one more thinking being on its surface, your homage to Nature, your humble gift in absolute gratitude for being alive yourself. When you give birth you realize this was the one thing you were called to do, this was the reason why your tiny body hosted hundreds of eggs in you for so long, this was worth the whole adventure it takes to find a compatible partner for a lifetime. And when they are about six weeks old and start actually reacting to you, cooing and looking you right in the eyes while you feed them, you realize all that work, the stitches, the night sweats, the back out of whack, and the wide waist, is all worth it. Every single thing you lost, name it: control over your life, time for yourself, a prosperous professional career, orgasms and trips to Bangkok, you would give up almost voluntarily because that little smile, that way they grip to you when you hold them, their tiny feet times four, are the best thing that has ever happened to you. Ever.

"What do you mean twins? You are baffled, overjoyed until you realize this is something you were not prepared for, how are you going to do this?"

124 | the end of the honeymoon

Chapter 27

The End of the Honeymoon

I don't want to be a mom anymore. I give up. The babies I used to adore are not here anymore. Those toddlers that used to drive me mad one second and rob my heart the next five, where did they go? Instead of adorable cuties, I have two rambunctious four year-olds who run, fight, shout, put their limbs in danger and my head on migraines. I used to tell them what to do, and normally they would do it because I am their mom. Now they don't do it for the same reason: I am their mom. I have become the one who tells them all the things they cannot do: don't wipe yourself on your shirt, don't dive under the stool when your brother is on top of it washing his hands, don't sit on the dog, don't run with the glass of water in your hand, don't push, don't, don't, don't. I hate being the "don't" person in his house. I want to sit and let them do whatever they want, let them run wild; let them like me because I am not nagging them.

I try my best to be a good mom, I teach them how to close their mouths while they eat, how to fold their pajamas, how to put their dishes in the dishwasher. I want them to become independent, so I sit with Rodrigo who wants to zip his own jacket for a good period of time teaching him how to. I offer Sebastián opportunities to burn all the bubbling energy, but it often ends up not being enough. If we go to the park, why are we leaving so early? (the fact that it is becoming freezing cold and the sun is going down seem to be no good reasons for them). If we go across the street to look at the impact hammer, why aren't we getting on it? (Because it is sitting across a huge ditch?) If we have ice cream for dessert, why can't we have a third serving? And so on. I am no longer their favorite person in the world, like when they were little and I was the source of the milk, the pacifier, the perfect toy. I used to know what they needed and I provided it. Now I am on their way, I am something that they'd rather live without; I am obstructing their path to perfect fun. Am I going to let them jump from the upper bunk bed? No. Am I going to let them go outside when it is 30 F° without mittens? No. Am I going to let them leave a public bathroom without washing their hands? No. So I get the "agh´s" and the rolling eyes, the mumbled words and the "but *Mami*...." in the whiniest voice ever. I cannot stand whiners, I am not going to raise brats, I refuse to have my kids sit at a table and sound like barn animals while they eat. Over my dead body. Am I asking for too much? Before, being a mom was a responsibility about basic needs, mostly related to keeping them alive and healthy: clothes, food, sleep. Now that their brains are no longer little--and I read it actually will not grow that much in the rest of their lives because the human brain reaches its full size at about six years of age, so that is less than fourteen months away for my kids--they question, they fight decisions, they try to find the tiniest little fault in the rules to get away with what they want. It is incredible how intelligent they can be when it comes to having their way.

Is my disappointment normal? Should I go to therapy? Am I joining another secret club that no one told me about? When I was pregnant I had no idea how hard it was to take care of a newborn, let alone two. But falling in love with them was the most fabulous experience in my life. Now that they are thinking jumping beans, I feel tricked because we were supposed to be this happy living family who would listen, respect and love each other. Half of the time my kids don't like me. One of them literally said the other night; "*Mami*, I like Daddy much gooder than you." I stood up, left the room and went to cry in the next one, I was completely taken aback. My baby does not like me? How did we come to this? He also tells me; "Stop saying that! I want my rules, not your rules!" He melts and makes a scene that I am not sure if I want to run and disappear forever or stay and face the fact that I am a mother of four year-old twins, for good and for bad. The bad sometimes hits hard, because they are incapable to see how lucky they are now. They have two parents alive, who have jobs and provide for more than their basic needs. Four fifths of the kids in this world are not that lucky. Do my kids care about that? Of course not, they are four for crying out loud! Do they know most kids have only one pair of pajamas and not two or three, and probably do not have to make a big deal about wearing the right one tonight? Did I go wrong and give too many choices when they were toddlers? Where did I go wrong?

Everywhere I go I get compliments about my kids. They behave, they listen, they follow instructions, one of them is funny, articulate, fast. The other is attentive, respectful, considerate. Their teachers love them. There is always someone at the grocery store who praises them because they help and stay close to me. When we fly, after landing, passengers come up to say "Wow, I didn't know there were kids on the plane!"

They say thank you, please, smile, give answers, and offer information. In the karate class they got a special recognition for being the only kids in their age group that do not need a special tutor assigned to them. In their first piano lesson today the teacher was complimenting them because they knew all their numbers and letters, and can actually read short words. I have no doubt they will become wonderful men in their lives, hopefully intelligent good human beings that find peace in their hearts and a passion that moves them to start everyday proud of themselves. But... am I going to be the casualty of that? Is our relationship going to be at risk starting now and at many other times as they grow? Will they have to go to psychotherapy to get rid of their memories of a controlling mother? Or am I raising obsessive kids, in a continuum of obsessive personalities in my family, so the tradition is not broken?

So where is my husband in all this? He is actually with me, on my side. He insists on discipline, in listening, and puts limits as much as I do. The difference, and this is a big one, is the time. Even though we are both professionals who work, because I am part time and work from home, I get to spend more time with the kids. Therefore, I get to yell more. I get more "don't do that" time with my kids. So when he comes home, he plays. He carries them; he juggles them in the air. He sometimes gets lenient when it comes to picking up dishes or putting on their own shoes. So they love him to death, and I don't mean only because of that, but in comparing him to me, they always choose him. They prefer his company, his car, his bathing them, his knees. I am the boring mom, the one of which they have too much in the day. And sometimes that is a relief, sometimes it is a bit of envy. Or both combined. A glimpse of what they will do in adolescence: let go of the mom, go be a man.

The great thing about being pregnant is that you spend nine months marveling at the wonder of you and your husband creating new life that is actually kicking underneath your skin. Then come the first years, with all the fabulous "firsts": first smile, first step, first word, first time tasting pears. Then come the fun years, when they are two and three and they ramble through the world discovering, making funny faces, clinging to you at times but wanting to run and be the conqueror, the sky is the limit, let's climb this chair, jump in the pool, kiss you with their lips still full of chocolate. Now I am in the "w---?" years, and some "why's" are great: why do the clouds move, why is the night dark, where is Brazil, what language do they speak in China, what is my middle name, why did you and daddy get married, why were you happy when you found out you had two babies and not only one in your belly, why don't all my friends at school have twins? I love those two inquisitive minds. I don't like the other w's though: why do we have to go? What time can we watch our video? Where is the rest of my Halloween candy? How come you get to make all the rules? They can't imagine I, myself, do not know the answer to this last question.

Since I refuse to become the "because I am your mother" phrase, and because we consciously decided not to spank or hit the children, I have to pay the price and use words, reasoning, logic... Which sometimes works, sometimes does not. Sometimes I have the answer, sometimes I don't and so they are left with my best effort. I guess that is what we are doing in this house in the end: nothing close to perfection, just our best effort. Let's just hope that will be enough.

"They question, they fight decisions, they try to find the tiniest little fault in the rules to get away with what they want."

Chapter 28

Fever

Yesterday Sebastián had fever all afternoon. When I went to pick him up from pre-school, the poor thing did not want to walk, he was cold, his cheeks were red. When I touched his forehead I realized he had a high fever. We came back home and he was burning. They watched videos; Rodrigo was happy because that is his favorite thing to do. I was hurrying up with work. I made Sebastián's favorite meal: albóndigas (meatballs), but he did not want to eat them. He only ate some chicken broth and orange sherbert. He vomited twice, arching and suffering, he hates throwing up. But he does not cry, instead, when he is done he typically says "I feel much better mami". I gave him a bath and fell asleep. All night the fever continued.

In the morning the tears were because I told him he could not go to pre-school because he was sick. Thick, quiet tears dripped down, as if I had told him he was never going back to school. Promises that we would watch his favorite videos or read his favorite books were not enough. He cried. My little one did not want to miss school, he wanted to play with his friends, be in classroom, sing his songs. But we could do nothing, and Rodrigo left all alone with his dad to go to school. I saw him leave alone, I saw Sebastián alone at home, and I realized that for the first time, they were going to be apart like this. David told me that when he dropped Rodrigo off, he looked so lonely, because none of his close friends went to school either – they must have been ill too. My heart shrinks when I see how they start facing life without their twin brother, without that pair who is always close, playing, fighting, sleeping, hesitating, teasing, and sometimes making cry. Without that other kid with whom they have lived since inception, since they were inside my belly, who they have seen fall, laugh, get hurt. That other kid who they will do anything for, like run inside the house to get the band aids, or try to comfort if they had a bad fall. And despite all this, at the end of their journey on our home, they will leave to face the world alone, with a brother very close by undoubtedly, but the world treats humans as individuals, not as pairs, and they will get a job, find a couple, their passion, their dreams. In reality, for me to talk about their relationship is a bit strange for two reasons. First, I am not a twin, and therefore I do not exactly know what it is to have a pair for life, of the same age, the same size, and discover the world together, share a mother and learn to share no matter what.

Second, because I only have twins. I have never had a singleton. Sometimes I wonder if it is easier to have only one. That way, there would be no competing for my attention, I would not need to explain things twice. In the playground, I would not need to have one eye on one and one eye on the other one at the same time, twice apprehensive and worried. I would not make the mistake of bathing the same baby twice. Sometimes I wonder if I had had a twin, it would have been fun. These two entertain each other with not much help, like if they had a little friend over every day. They also have the best translator in each other – when I don't understand what one is saying, the other one intervenes and explains to me what his twin is trying to say.

There is one thing that is clear through all this: the relationship Rodrigo and Sebastián have is the strongest one of their lives. Despite the typical fight for the toy or for who gets to wash hands first, in between them there is this link which is so pervasive that is almost physical. Stronger than anything I can even imagine.

"Despite the typical fight for the toy or for who gets to wash hands first, in between them there is this link which is so pervasive that is almost physical. Stronger than anything I can even imagine."

Chapter 29: Don't Grow

It is a little bit after midnight on a Monday night in winter. It is 4°F, -16°F, outside. Before going to bed, I went to see the kids sleeping. The night light hit Sebastián's face just so that I had to kneel down and see him, admire him in his deep, baby-like sleep. His mouth was half open, his eyes completely shut, his skin glowed like yellow porcelain. I sat on the floor and just watched him. Not a sound, just their breathing. In the upper bunk bed, Rodrigo slept, but I, with my forty years, refuse to climb and risk a bad back only because I want to see him sleeping. With Rodrigo, I just listen, although I do see him every morning sleeping, since he comes to our bed at 4 AM, of course. I did not want to move from staring at Sebastián. It was such a fascinating view that I finally understood all those artists who tried to catch that devotion in the paintings of of mothers looking at their babies.

All mothers, we all look that way to our children at some point, with adoration, worship... and suddenly, from the bottom of my heart, I heard myself murmuring; "Don't grow, please don't grow." I had the urge to tell him: Please stay like this; little, gorgeous, energetic. Don't learn about war, don't ask about poverty, don't see any of those violent video games where there is killing, blood, and aggression. Don't grow, keep being naïve, keep thinking I am the best mom and daddy is the strongest dad, keep asking me to come with you if it is too dark, keep listening attentively while I read to you. Stay like you are, a wonderful little boy that believes in magic, in Santa, in *Los Santos Reyes*. I would prefer if you did not have to learn about capital punishment, about how many illiterate children exist today in the world, about how many die of hunger while other countries send million-dollar missions to see if there is water in Mars. Keep playing with trains; keep getting excited about us building a fire truck out of a huge cardboard box, with wheels that we paint and ladders made out of pieces of wood. Don't wake up one day and pass by me without saying like you say today "Good morning *Mami*, today is a school day, yeah!" Don't learn about human trafficking or crack babies.

But if you have to grow (and you will), grow strong. It is your destiny to keep growing, I cannot stop it, I should not. I know I must be a bad mother if I don't want you to grow, and I want you to, I do, only that I have this stupid desire to put a bubble around you and have you live in a world where there are only good intentions and people with good hearts live. Because that is what you believe the world is today, and who are we –the adults—to destroy your reality? What power is invested in us to demolish the notion that everyone loves each other? Please don't stop humming Christmas songs, and keep singing to me while I cook, that funny song that says "My hair had a party last night," and when we see someone having a bad hair day, you smile and whisper to me: "*Mami*, his hair had a party last night!" and you giggle but try not to be obvious because you know that peoples' feelings can be hurt.

Don't grow, I am begging you, don't learn bad words, don't fight with other kids, don't get offended when someone says you are short or you were not first in the race. Keep thinking we are all the same, we all have great intentions, and we really can like each other. Keep being oblivious to people's skin color and accents. Keep learning something new every day, keep that need to understand why the sun comes up by the kitchen and goes down by the living room, why ice melts, what it is to vote. Keep being a happy kid, whose only problems are that the choice of afternoon snack is apple and not donuts. A part of me does want to see you grow. I want you to understand how the moon's phases change, and how the Maya built a gorgeous stone observatory, I want you to see the Danube, to dance in the Rio carnival, to attend an opening of the Olympics. I want you to fall madly and hopelessly in love, to defend your opinion, to stand up for someone who is too frail to defend himself. I would love it if you swam in a *cenote* in Yucatán. One day you will read the Hindu legends about kings, adventures, full of symbolisms and hope. I would really enjoy seeing you excel at what you like to do, finding your core, feeling free, and enjoying life because that is what life is for.

In the meantime, tonight, I don't want you to grow. I don't want you to learn about the evil that exists or the tragedies that are suffered by millions everyday. But I cannot help it, and I must face that your body will continue getting taller and your brain more complex. I wish you the best in that journey; I will be right here, kneeling at your side while you sleep, holding your hand, and staying away when you need me to do so too. I am certain you will become a man that shares what is good in his heart, because your heart is the biggest part of you already.

"I had the urge to tell him:
Please stay like this;
little, gorgeous, energetic."

Chapter 30
Gracias

How do you thank someone for teaching your kids to be respectful to others? How do you give thanks for looking after your kids and allowing them to have a blast? Sebastián and Rodrigo come home with treasures in their hands: large watercolor sheets with designs that speak to the joy they feel at pre-school and to their ability to express themselves through lines and texture. They bring me invitations to Mother's Day celebrations. They talk incessantly about their day, who came today, who was missing, who rang the bell, who was the train leader, how a quarrel was solved, and if the playground was dusty or wet. I live through them the immense glory that is to be little in size and enormous in imagination. As they get on their booster seats they are like bubbles of energy, atoms spinning around at unbelievable speed, whirling around their morning at pre-school. They enjoy their friends so much, and beg for play dates (like they don't see them all morning!). Therefore, sometimes we go have pizza with Joe, who was referred to the other day like this by Sebastián: "Joe and me are best friends, we love each other... well, Joe, Rodrigo and me, we love each other so much!" Notice how the dynamics of twins came in the middle of the phrase, because thou shall not forget thy twin, seems to be the founding stone of all twin relationships.

When I go to their classroom to read a book in Spanish or help with a craft, I see their friends, all little and adorable gnomes alike, full of smiles, funny as can be. The things these kids say could fill out a bestseller humor book. But also their comments house great wisdom, like Rodrigo this morning: "... on the Flipper movie, remember? The bad guy killed Flipper's mommy... but that was just a movie, right? Because who would kill a dolphin? No one would kill a dolphin, right *Mami*?" So then, the hardest moments of parenthood arise and you are caught between two worlds: should I tell my kid that in reality, there are people who shoot dolphins for fun? Or should I tell him that no one in their right mind and heart could kill an innocent dolphin? Moments like these are starting to happen more often, and I am afraid they will never stop. So when they have Earth Week at pre-school and they come home stating throwing garbage is not good for the planet and one yells to the other: "Stop wasting water! You are taking too long washing your hands," where do you start saying "Thank you" to the teachers at pre-school? Because teaching is beyond recognizing and reciting 1, 2, 3's and A, B, C's. Anyone can teach that. But true teaching, I have come to learn in this pre-school, is about relating to each other, about connecting to their environment, and I am lucky that my two kids go to this great pre-school, where their teachers have helped me model them, carve them into better little human beings. And when Rodrigo and Sebastián come in carrying a sculpture made of wood pieces, glued together with five-year-old mastery, each one astonishingly resembling their own personalities, in silence I send a thanks to their teachers, who allow my kids to feel free when they create, giving me a lesson about being non-directive and accepting them for what they are: two little persons with hearts of giants and ingenuity galore.

"... because who would kill a dolphin? No one would kill a dolphin, right *Mami*?"

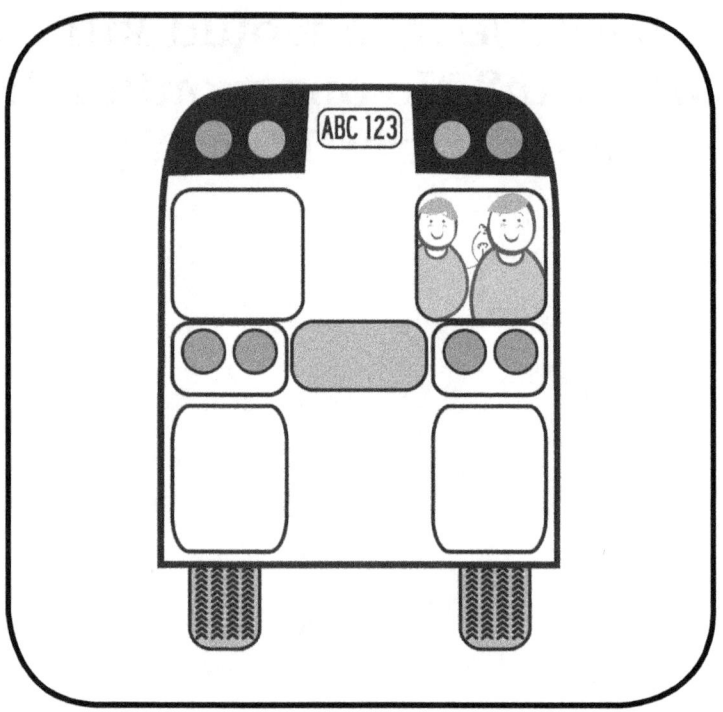

Chapter 31
Going to Kindergarten

David and I just finished filling out kindergarten registration forms. We faced the seven different forms (David did Sebastián's, I did Rodrigo's), some of which were absolutely necessary and others redundant. If I were given this set of documents to form an opinion of the school my kids are going to attend, it would not be a very good one. We had to write the same information seven times for seven different departments at the school like registrar, nurse office, transportation, etc.

We had to answer some dumb ones in the case of twins like:

Does your child play with others his or her own age? Yes or No.
Are they the older, younger or the same age?

Beneath all this blabbering, a high tide of anxiety overwhelms me: my twins are going to kindergarten in five months. They will be putting on their backpacks and getting on a bus. I will be the supportive mother who smiles while waving bye-bye. I don't know if I am elated or petrified. Elated to see them grow, happy, energetic, full of curiosity. Petrified because this is just the beginning of a bigger step they are taking into the world, a world that is not our house, our controlled environment. They will go out there and see the good and the bad. It might be that lately I have been forced to pessimism from hints of the outside.

Last week as I was walking past a classroom in a church building, I saw a flipchart that had obviously been used for some kind of religious teaching which read: the pros of the Jews are (listed 2), and the cons of the Jews are: Jews killed Jesus. I could not read any further. I froze. How can anyone in their right mind be writing (let alone teaching!) this? To whom? Obviously they were lacking a significant amount of neurons, but the frightening fact was that it was there, written, in black and white, as a silent testimony that someone out there still portrays Jews as not really good people. If this were happening seventy years ago in a country in Europe, I would understand (not agree though) how historically it could happen, but for crying out loud, it is the XXI century and we live in a supposedly civilized country, where people actually get to go to school... but apparently some of those schools should really just not exist. I realized how strong religious faith can go into society. That written phrase talked to me about a whole philosophy of life, about a lot of people that I do not know. Clearly there are people who live close to my house who think their religion makes them superior to others.

The other thing that happened to me just today was that while driving to the grocery store I saw an old car with a sticker that read: Marriage=man+woman. This seemed pretty obvious until a split second after I read it I fell into the real message that marriage is not for homosexuals. The driver of this old car was a young man, clean cut, very muscular and showing off, one of those that if they could, they would show you how big their penis is if you'd just let them. I am convinced deep inside every macho man, resides a scared boy. Then the light turned green and he drove off while I turned left. I wanted to follow him and tell him his sticker was wrong. I wanted to catch up and ask him how dare anyone put a sticker like that on their car? But... when I recently wrote on my dirty car: No To War, I bet some people were just as upset as I was today against this driver.

The last thing that got me pessimistic was a sign in the local civic center, announcing right after "Kids Expo," the "NRA Banquet." Again, I have to apologize for not understanding this, probably because where I grew up all guns are controlled and the local supermarket does not sell bullets. "NRA Banquet" seemed to me a big contradiction: how can people who like guns have a party? Is killing something to celebrate? A banquet to me is a big dinner to commemorate something. The National Rifle Association is the synonym of death in my mind. For some reason I don't buy into all their arguments, about hunting for sport and self-defense. Maybe it was a mistake and the banquet was to celebrate those members of the NRA were giving up their guns, making sure they were destroyed and not re-sold, and were embracing a life of peace and contemplation. Hey, you have to keep the faith, right?

You can see by my writing that I am trying to avoid by all means the fact that today we took the first step to see our kids go to school. Formal school. School with a capital S. Not pre-school, the semi-playgroup they attend now. It happily coincided with the same day we had our conference with the teachers at pre-school, who told us how marvelous the kids are, what a joy to have them in the class, how considerate, sensitive and amazing with numbers Rodrigo is, and how outspoken, participative, energetic Sebastián is. "It is obvious your parenting skills are excellent because we can see Sebastián and Rodrigo come from a home full of love, attention, boundaries, they listen, they tell stories, they play so well with others." Truth or not, talk about an ego-booster. I walked out of there thinking I am a pretty good mom apparently. But am I good enough to teach my kids that gays have equal rights, that violence is never the right way, that faith should never be a reason for hate?

As I was filling out this registration form, I realized my role as a mom is going to be to let them go every day a little more. Today I know what they are wearing, what they eat, who they play with, (mostly) what happened at pre-school, if they have a cough and what toy they broke. Semi-complete lock of mother and child, separate yet very close, and not as engulfing as the relationship with a toddler or a baby. In fifteen years though, I might hear from them when and if they call me from wherever they are. I will have no idea what they do in the day, nor control over their thoughts, friends, decisions, or love lives. They will be adults, and I will be the mother of those adults. People will ask me "do you have kids?" and I will answer "I don't have kids, I have adults". Hopefully those adults will look at others beyond race, religion or sexual preference; they would have learned to see past those attributes and learn to respect others, without necessarily agreeing with everyone, and will be at peace with themselves and others..

Sebastián is now in a phase where he calls me "my sweetheart" as he runs to hug me and kiss me. Rodrigo slept with me in our bed because his cough was so bad all night long, and held my hand while asleep. I have a feeling that I am going to miss this as years go by. But today they are still here, they are still little and I must enjoy them as much as I can.

Afterword

The boys are older now and life is different. As I look back and re-read the chapters in this book I feel nostalgic... but mostly exhausted! How did we do this? Seems like the Sofía I was then was obsessed with her kids, totally immersed in motherhood with no time for much else. It is so interesting how being a mom can be so demanding, yet many of us would do it all over again without hesitation. I believe parenthood is like a good kiss: you can read all about it, but it is not until you kiss that you realize what it is all really about. Once a friend asked me: what is it like to be a mother? The truth is words are not meant to explain things like that. And in reality, everyone's experience is different. One thing is universal though: the love a parent feels for his or her child. It does not matter if you live in a slum, in a mansion, if you went to school, if you are employed or not. The love a parent feels is independent of religion, country, language, political view, personal preferences. In that way, having kids is like joining this ancestral chain of beings that hold the biggest secret of all: nothing renders you more human than creating life. When you have twins, multiply that by two. And that is why, after you have twins, you are left almost literally 'seeing double'.

www.ingramcontent.com/pod-product-compliance
Lightning Source LLC
Chambersburg PA
CBHW051805040426
42446CB00007B/522